ARROWSMITH

NOTES

including
Introduction
Chapter Summaries and Commentaries
Critical Notes
Character Sketches
Study Questions and Theme Topics
Bibliography

D1922394

by

Salibelle Royster
Evansville College

editor
Gary Carey, M.A.
University of Colorado

consulting editor
James L. Roberts, Ph.D.
Department of English
University of Nebraska

Cliffs Notes®
INCORPORATED
LINCOLN, NEBRASKA 68501

ISBN 0-8220-0201-9
© Copyright 1964
by
C. K. Hillegass
All Rights Reserved
Printed in U.S.A.

CONTENTS

INTRODUCTION

Sinclair Lewis considered several titles over a period of months before deciding on *Arrowsmith* for his novel about the medical profession. Some of those discarded were *The Stumbler, The Barbarian* or just *Barbarian, Martin Arrowsmith, M.D., Dr. Martin, Martin,* and even *Doc*. The last, suggested by his publisher, Alfred Harcourt, of Harcourt Brace, was dismissed as too informal, *Martin* and *Dr. Martin* as too "sentimental-lady-novelistish," and the one containing reference to the medical degree as "too much of a mouthful." The final choice of *Arrowsmith* was a happy one, since it is both brief and dignified and is well adapted both to the book and the motion picture based on it. Because of the existence in England of a publishing house called Arrowsmith, Lewis's British publishers used the title *Dr. Martin Arrowsmith.* It is not unusual for the same book to appear under different titles on the two sides of the Atlantic.

Written in collaboration with Dr. Paul de Kruif, formerly on the staff of Rockefeller Institute for Medical Research and himself an eminent scientist of the era, *Arrowsmith* is precise and authentic in medical detail. Sinclair Lewis came from a family of doctors, both his father and his brother Claude being physicians. Hence a novel based on scientific research played a significant role in Lewis's career as an author, winning for him the Pulitzer Prize in Literature in 1926, an honor which he refused to accept. It is considered Lewis's masterpiece, for in addition to being his best creative work, it reflects the life and experiences of the author to a greater degree than any of his other books.

There are two versions of *Arrowsmith,* the serialized one appearing under the British title, *Dr. Martin Arrowsmith,* shorter and less detailed than the other, with less scientific background. The version on which this study guide is based is the longer one. Although the book is discussed at some length, the guide is merely an aid to the understanding of the novel itself and is to be used in conjunction with, not as a substitute for, the reading of the book.

SINCLAIR LEWIS AND THE AMERICAN SCENE

On January 10, 1951, Sinclair Lewis died in a clinic on the outskirts of Rome, less than a month before his sixty-sixth birthday. In thirty-seven years he had written twenty-one novels, many short stories, a few plays, and some poetry on varied themes.

Best known for his novels, Lewis wrote several unsuccessful ones, *Our Mr. Wrenn, The Trail of the Hawk, The Job, The Innocents,* and *Free Air,* before attaining national recognition with *Main Street,* published in October, 1920. This story of Carol Kennicott and her reaction to Gopher Prairie and its inhabitants stabilized Lewis's reputation as a writer of realistic fiction and a portrayer of the American scene. *Main Street* was followed two years later by *Babbitt,* whose name became a symbol for the conformist and unidealistic businessman. *Arrowsmith,* published in 1925, marked the peak of Lewis's career.

Sinclair Lewis's birthplace is Sauk Centre, Minnesota. On February 7, 1885, the third son of Dr. Edwin J. Lewis and Emma Kermott Lewis was born there. Mrs. Lewis was of Canadian and English descent. The Lewis ancestors came from New York state, being descended from Welsh miners and Yorkshiremen. Dr. Lewis's mother, Emiline Johnson, was reputedly a direct descendant of Peregrine White, first white child born in New England (1620-1704) of Mayflower and Plymouth Plantation stock. Of the three sons in Dr. Lewis's family, only the eldest, Fred, did not attain distinction. Dr. Claude Lewis, the second son, was an eminent surgeon, and his younger brother, Harry Sinclair, later known as "Red", of course received world-wide acclaim for his writing of fiction.

When young Harry was six years old, his mother died. He had inherited her facial features and apparently a good deal of her temperament. He did not take kindly to his stepmother, Isabel Warner Lewis, who he felt treated him like a child.

Sauk Centre, Minnesota, was in the 1880's a bare, unlovely town only thirty years old, which did not become a city until 1889.

The year of Sinclair Lewis's birth the population of the village and town combined was 2807. Surrounded by prairie farming land dotted with thirty of Minnesota's ten thousand lakes, the town was nevertheless drab and uninviting. In summer the temperature might rise to 110 degrees; in winter it might dip to 40 below zero.

An indifferent, poorly adjusted, and awkward youngster, Harry Lewis was seventeenth in a class of eighteen in the eighth grade. At the age of thirteen he tried to enlist as a drummer boy in the Spanish-American War but was promptly apprehended by his father. In high school he improved, taking part in debating and other forms of public speaking. In 1903, when he was in the academy of Oberlin College preparing for Yale, he described himself as "Tall, ugly, thin, red-haired, but not, methinks, especially stupid." He was a misfit at Yale, although he was editor of *Literary Magazine* and worked on New Haven newspapers. He dropped out of college before graduation.

After more than a year of temporary jobs, including editing, writing children's verses for magazines, and going to Panama by steerage in search of work on the canal, he returned to Yale in 1907 and received his degree in 1908. Well-read in the English classics and experienced in free lance writing, Lewis held during the next four years positions as editor, reporter, manuscript reader, advertising manager, and reviewer. His first novel, *Hike and the Aeroplane,* published under the pseudonym of "Tom Graham," appeared in 1912, to be followed in 1914 by *Our Mr. Wrenn,* the year of his marriage to Grace Livingstone Hegger.

This marriage, detailed by the first Mrs. Lewis in *Half a Loaf* and *With Love from Gracie,* was to last fourteen years, until the divorce in 1928. This period of time included the birth of a son, Wells, born in 1917 and killed by a sniper in Alsace during World War II (1944). These years also embraced Lewis's rise to fame, beginning with the publishing of his earlier novels, *The Trail of the Hawk, The Job, The Innocents,* and *Free Air* and reaching a high level in 1920 with the appearance of *Main Street.*Other successful volumes followed: *Babbitt* (1922); *Arrowsmith* (1925); *Elmer Gantry* (1927); *The Man Who Knew Coolidge* (1928); and *Dods-*

worth (1929). Lewis declined the Pulitzer Prize for *Arrowsmith,* as he did not feel that it represented the more favorable side of American life and culture. Being a realist, he wanted to be free to criticize rather than to flatter.

After his divorce from his first wife, Lewis married Dorothy Thompson, widely known foreign correspondent and newspaper columnist. The next year (1929) *Dodsworth* was published, and Lewis began research on a labor novel, which was never to be completed, despite repeated efforts. The year 1930 marked the birth of Lewis's second son, Michael, and the awarding of the coveted Nobel Prize for Literature for *Babbitt.* This time Lewis accepted the prize, which amounted to almost $50,000. He had won, whether deservedly or not, over such literary giants as Theodore Dreiser, Joseph Hergesheimer, Upton Sinclair, and two women novelists who were literary artists: Ellen Glasgow, an American, and Rebecca West, of England. Lewis traveled to Stockholm to receive the prize, the first American writer to be thus honored. The next was to be Eugene O'Neill, whose dramas won it six years later. This was a fitting climax to Lewis's great decade, the 1920's, beginning with *Main Street* and ending with the highest recognition in the literary world.

Lewis's excesses, including heavy drinking, shortened his life, according to his brother, Dr. Claude Lewis, but apparently they did not affect his writing. The twenties, peak years of the Lewis career, were an era of prohibition, jazz, big business, speakeasies, bathtub gin, and general recklessness – an aftermath of World War I. The grand climax was the stock market crash of 1929 and the subsequent great depression of the 1930's. The year 1933 brought repeal of prohibition, breadlines, and joblessness, when Boston Common was black with the recumbent bodies of unemployed men. Franklin Delano Roosevelt became president in 1933 and remained in office until his death in 1945. Lewis declined in popularity, although the process was slow.

Ann Vickers appeared in 1933 and *It Can't Happen Here,* written as a result of his knowledge of conditions abroad, particularly in Germany, on which his wife, Dorothy Thompson, was an authority, was published in 1936. That year Sinclair Lewis was also awarded an honorary degree at Yale. In 1938 *The Prodigal Parents* appeared and a play, *Angela Is Twenty-two,* in which Lewis himself acted. In 1942 he and Dorothy Thompson were divorced, after a separation of nearly five years. Lewis later became involved with a young actress, Marcella Powers.

Lewis continued to write novels throughout the 1940's: *Gideon Planish* (1943); *Cass Timberlane* (1945); *Kingsblood Royal* (1947); *The God-seeker* (1949); and *World So Wide* (1951), the year of his death. His ashes were returned for burial at Sauk Centre. His famous divorced wife, Dorothy Thompson, outlived him by ten years, dying in Lisbon in 1961.

Such was the career of Sinclair Lewis, who held the mirror up to the American scene of the first half of the twentieth century, showing "scorn her own image, and the very age and body of the time his form and pressure."*

**Hamlet,* III-ii-26-27

PAUL DE KRUIF'S PART IN *ARROWSMITH*

Sinclair Lewis met Dr. Paul de Kruif (pronounced dē krif) through another well-known physician, Dr. Morris Fishbein. De Kruif had taken a Ph.D in bacteriology from the University of Michigan and had then become a researcher at Rockefeller Institute, only to lose his appointment when he published *Our Medical Men,* a book critical of the profession. On their way back from a midnight visit to Eugene Debs, the labor leader, whom Lewis admired, Fishbein questioned Lewis's plan to write a novel about labor, with Debs as the model for the hero. At that time or shortly after, Lewis and De Kruif agreed to work together on a novel about medical science, with a doctor as protagonist and a plague in the Caribbean as an important episode. They decided to make a research tour together to the West Indies and to continue to Europe to write the novel.

They sailed from New York to the West Indies January 4, 1923. A contract was drawn up for a full collaboration, Lewis to receive seventy-five per cent of the royalty and De Kruif twenty-five. De Kruif received a ten-thousand-dollar advance and before leaving married a former student, Rhea Barbarin, thought to be the original of Leora.

De Kruif was a powerful man at this time and had great physical vitality. Without his help *Arrowsmith* could never have been written, for he was an expert. Lewis could only draw on early experiences as the youngest member of a medical family. The sea voyage lasted two months and included the Lesser Antilles and a part of Barbados, where the chief medical officer guided Lewis and De Kruif through hospitals, almshouses, and a leper asylum. They visited the bacteriological laboratory in Panama. Lewis wrote to H. G. Wells: "With me is Paul de Kruif, the bacteriologist... a man with a knife-edge mind and an iconoclasm that really means something." To H. L. Mencken Lewis wrote: "The book goes grand. Paul de Kruif proves to have as much synthetic fictional imagination as he has scientific knowledge." The only arguments the pair had in a month and a half were a part of Lewis's research, when he would bait De Kruif with questions and criticize and deride the answers. They even observed the men around them for physical types and found Arrowsmith himself, "a grave, black-haired youngster looking at us... in the ship's smoking room."

In England De Kruif introduced Lewis to many medical scientists and into laboratories and clinics in the London area. The book progressed, and De Kruif was enthusiastic about the first draft. The friendship between the collaborators broke up, however, over the acknowledgement of De Kruif's part in the writing of *Arrowsmith.* "In collaboration with Paul de Kruif" was the phrase to appear in small type on the title page or on a page following. Lewis proposed to insert an extended statement of paragraph length. De Kruif finally accepted, but from that time on he lost interest in the book. Several years later, however, he did give assistance for the scenario.

De Kruif is an author in his own right, having produced many magazine articles on medical subjects and several books. He once referred to himself as "a sort of anti-microbe missionary." Some of his best-known books are *The Microbe Hunters, Hunger Fighters,* and *Men Against Death.*

LIST OF CHARACTERS WITH IDENTIFICATION

Major

Martin Arrowsmith, M.D., scientist and leading character
Leora Tozer Arrowsmith, Martin's first wife
Dr. Max Gottlieb, professor of bacteriology and true scientist

Minor but Important

Dr. Terry Wickett, Martin's associate in scientific research
Madeline Fox, to whom Martin at one time is engaged
Joyce Lanyon Arrowsmith, Martin's second wife
Gustaf Sondelius, colorful Swedish physician and lecturer

Others

Doc Vickerson, who first inspired Martin to want to study medicine

Faculty of Winnemac

Professor Edward Edwards, head of department of chemistry
Dr. Norman Brumfit, instructor in English
Dr. T. J. H. ("Dad") Silva, dean of the medical school
Dr. John Aldington Robertshaw, professor of physiology
Dr. Oliver O. Stout, professor of anatomy
Dr. Lloyd Davidson, professor of *materia medica*
Dr. Roscoe Geake, professor of otolaryngology
Dr. Loiseau, professor of surgery
Dr. Horace Greeley Truscott, president of the university

Members of Digamma Pi

Reverend Ira Hinkley, desirous of becoming a missionary
Clif Clawson, the class jester
Angus Duer, brilliant, hard-driving valedictorian of his class

"Fatty" Pfaff, the butt of many crude jokes
Irving Watters, a serious second-year medic.

Mrs. Fox, Madeline's mother
Nelly Byers, probationary nurse, friend of Leora
"Dr." Benoni Carr, a charlatan
Dr. Rouncefield, head of the Chicago clinic
George F. Babbitt, Zenith real estate king
Dr. Entwisle, a youngish physiologist from Harvard
Dawson Hunziker, president of Hunziker pharmaceutical firm
Mrs. Gottlieb, peasant wife of the great scientist
Robert Gottlieb, their worthless son
Miriam Gottlieb, their faithful daughter
Another Gottlieb daughter (unnamed) who eloped with a gambler

People of Wheatsylvania and Its Environs

Andrew Jackson Tozer, Leora's father
Mrs. Tozer, Leora's mother
Bert Tozer, brother of Leora
Ada Quist, fiancée of Bert
Mr. and Mrs. Norblom
Pete Yesta, so-called druggist
Alec Ingleblad, the barber
Miss Agnes Ingleblad, his aunt and housekeeper
Nils Krag, the carpenter
"Wise the Polack," a Russian Jew
Mr. and Mrs. Henry Novak
Mary Novak, their child
Dr. Adam Winter, elderly physician of Leopolis
Dr. Hesselink, of Groningen
Dr. and Mrs. Coughlin, of Leopolis
Dr. and Mrs. Tromp
Dr. Woestijne, health officer of Vanderheide's Grove
The seamstress, a typhoid carrier

People of Nautilus, Iowa

Dr. Almus Pickerbaugh, Director of the Department of Public Health

Mrs. Pickerbaugh, his wife
Their eight daughters: Orchid, Verbena, Daisy, Jonquil, Hibisca, Narcissa, Arbuta, and Gladiola
Old Klopchuk, owner of the local dairy
Dr. J. C. Long, brought in from Chicago to inspect the dairy
Clay Tredgold, president of Steel Windmill Company
Clara Tredgold, his wife
Mr. Schlemihl, president of Cornbelt Insurance Company
Mrs. Schlemihl, his wife
Dr. Bissex, football coach and professor of hygiene
Mayor Pugh, Pickerbaugh's political chief
Mr. F. X. Jordan, a contractor interested in politics
Dr. Rufus Ockford, Martin's assistant
Mrs. McCandless, owner of unfit dwellings
Monte Mugford, of the Ashford Grove group

People Connected with McGurk Institute, New York

Dr. Rippleton Holabird, head of the department of physiology
Mrs. Holabird, his wife
Miss Pearl Robbins, secretary to Dr. Tubbs
Dr. Nicholas Yeo, head of the department of biology
Dr. William T. Smith, assistant in biochemistry
Dr. Aaron Sholtheis, head of the department of epidemiology
Ross McGurk, chairman of the board, McGurk Institute
Mrs. Capitola McGurk, his wife
Dr. A. DeWitt Tubbs, director of McGurk Institute
Mrs. Tubbs, his wife
Dr. Gillingham, chief in biophysics
Raymond Pearl, the biometrician

People of St. Hubert, West Indies

Colonel Sir Robert Fairlamb, Governor of St. Hubert
Mrs. Evelyn Fairlamb, his wife
Hon. Cecil Twyford, influential critic of Sir Robert
Twyford's mother and five sons
Kellett the Red Leg, owner of a shipping company
George William Vertigan, owner of the Blue Bazaar

Dr. Inchcape Jones, the Surgeon General
Dr. Stokes, medical officer of St. Swithin Parish
Dr. Oliver Marchand, Negro physician of Blackwater

Still Others
Miss Gwilliam, a cultured tourist
Mr. S. Sanborn Hibble of Detroit, and Mrs. Dawson of Memphis, more shipboard acquaintances of Martin
Latham Ireland, wealthy New York lawyer, admirer of Joyce
John Arrowsmith, child of Martin and Joyce

DIGEST OF *ARROWSMITH*

Sinclair Lewis divides the novel into several sections or episodes, each with a change of scene, background, and often characters.

TRAINING OF A PHYSICIAN-SCIENTIST

Martin Arrowsmith, of pioneer descent and unflagging spirit, begins his medical training by reading Gray's *Anatomy* at the age of fourteen in the office of Doc Vickerson, of Elk Mills. In 1904 he enters Winnemac University, where during his career as a student he becomes assistant to Max Gottlieb, a German-Jew scientist, whom Martin deeply admires and respects. Digamma Pi is the fraternity through which Martin becomes acquainted with other students who are to reappear later in the story, notably Clif Clawson, Ira Hinkley, Angus Duer, and Irving Watters. During his years at Winnemac Martin falls in love with a probationary nurse, Leora Tozer, and marries her a year before graduation in Wheatsylvania, North Dakota. With the financial help of her unwilling family, they return to Winnemac, and Martin receives his M.D. degree, becoming an intern in Zenith General Hospital.

PRACTICE IN WHEATSYLVANIA

His internship over, Martin opens an office in Wheatsylvania, Leora's home town, and does general practice for two years. Always, however, his heart is in laboratory work.

Max Gottlieb loses his position on the faculty of Winnemac and joins the Hunziker Pharmaceutical Company of Pittsburgh, an institution criticized for unethical practices. Martin is disappointed that his former professor has formed such an alliance. The Tozer family and the general unpleasant surroundings cause Martin to welcome a chance to move on. This chance comes through his acquaintance with Dr. Gustaf Sondelius, Swedish physician and lecturer, who helps the young man obtain a position in Nautilus.

YEARS IN NAUTILUS

Martin's director in Nautilus, a town of seventy thousand, is Dr. Almus Pickerbaugh, head of the Department of Public Health, whose family consists of his wife and eight daughters. The oldest, Orchid, greatly admires the young physician. Martin is disappointed however, when he learns that a load of trivial duties will almost exclude any intensive laboratory work. In Nautilus Dr. Irving Watters, formerly of Digamma Pi, is now a leading practitioner.

Pickerbaugh is nominated for Congress, and Martin takes charge of the Department while the candidate is campaigning. Pickerbaugh is elected, and his leaving for Washington is celebrated lavishly. Martin, too eager to free the town of rats, fleas, and disease, incurs the disfavor of the authorities and is practically forced to resign. He writes to Angus Duer in Chicago.

IN CHICAGO

Duer, now a highly successful surgeon, employs Martin in Rouncefield Clinic. For a year he is an impersonal part of a large organization. Then an article which he publishes in a medical journal attracts the attention of Max Gottlieb, now a research scientist at McGurk Institute in New York. He offers Martin a position in laboratory work, which the young man accepts.

IN NEW YORK

Gottlieb advises Martin to study mathematics and physical chemistry in order to prove his own experiments. On the McGurk staff are also Dr. Rippleton Holabird, status-seeking head of the department of physiology; Dr. Terry Wickett, a rude and irritating seeker for scientific truth; and Dr. Tubbs, Director of the Institute.

America enters World War I in 1917, and work at the Institute is diverted to the war effort. Gottlieb is unkindly treated because of his German background.

Martin's experiments with laboratory cultures are dramatic. He discovers an X Principle, which will fight and control a number of diseases. A French scientist, D'Herelle, of Pasteur Institute in Paris, has made the same discovery, however, and his results are publicized before Martin's. Consequently Martin loses the credit and can only corroborate the findings of D'Hérelle.

THE WEST INDIES

A year passes before the bubonic plague breaks out in St. Hubert, an island in the West Indies. Sondelius reappears, and joins the staff of McGurk. He and Martin become collaborators in search of a cure for the plague. They are appointed by the Institute to go to St. Hubert and experiment with the *phage*. Leora insists on going along. Sondelius is to be charge of sanitation, and Martin is to do the actual testing. Both have explicit instructions from Gottlieb as to their procedures.

Conditions are much worse than expected on St. Hubert. Martin wishes that he had forced Leora to stay behind. He conducts his experiment but loses Leora and Sondelius, both of whom die of the plague. Ira Hinkley, who reappears in the West Indies, is also a victim. At the home of an official, Martin meets Joyce Lanyon, who is later to become his second wife. The plague is halted, and Martin returns to New York alone, where he is received with much acclaim by the press, the Public Health Service, and, of course, McGurk Institute.

CONCLUDING CHAPTERS

Martin's subsequent marriage to Joyce Lanyon brings him into a social world where the emphasis is on money and position rather than on search for truth. After several years of the marriage, during which a son, John Arrowsmith, is born, Martin leaves Joyce to join Terry Wickett in the Vermont hills, where, with a few other research men they can pursue their laboratory work in seclusion and peace. Joyce will probably divorce her husband and marry Latham Ireland, a friend of her first husband, Roger Lanyon. So ends the story of *Arrowsmith*.

CHAPTER I

I

Summary

In a flashback fifteen lines long, Sinclair Lewis recites an episode from the life of the great-grandmother of his hero, Martin Arrowsmith. As a motherless girl of fourteen, the great-grandmother has chosen to go on westward in a wagon with her sick father and her tattered brothers and sisters rather than to return to their relatives in Cincinnati.

Commentary

This introductory episode brings out the unflagging will power, the courage, and the spirit of adventure possessed by ancestors of the hero of the novel, Martin Arrowsmith. These characteristics are also apparent in the great-grandson, who is to show the pioneering spirit in his own field, medicine. This brief incident arouses interest in the reader and makes him wish to go on with the story.

II

Summary

Fourteen-year-old Martin Arrowsmith, son of the owner of the New York Clothing Bazaar, is reading Gray's *Anatomy* in Doc Vickerson's office in Elk Mills, in the state of Winnemac. The year is 1897. Martin is the unpaid assistant of Doc and takes charge of the office whenever Doc makes a call. Although Martin reads steadily all afternoon from the section on the lymphatic system, he also enjoys exhibiting to his gang the dreadful and fascinating skeleton with one gold tooth when Doc is absent.

Doc Vickerson's three ill-kept rooms – one of them his office – are on the second floor of the building also containing the New York Bazaar. They are a challenge and a "lure to questioning and adventure" for Martin Arrowsmith.

Commentary

This short section introduces not only the hero, as a teen-ager already a devotee of medical science, but also the slatternly, drunken, but dedicated Doc Vickerson, the first of numerous medical men who are to influence the life of Martin Arrowsmith. The sordid, unsanitary office and living quarters are described with Sinclair Lewis's own brand of realism. The characters are also true to life.

III

Summary

Although Doc Vickerson is sober upon his return, he does not remain so long. Thrice gurgles of Jamaica rum make him garrulous. He commends his young assistant for reading Gray and advises him to "get training" in basic science in order to become a "leadin' physician" earning five thousand dollars a year. Wishing to give Martin something to start his training, Doc holds out his beloved magnifying glass, used for years in botanizing, and watches the boy slip the lens into his pocket.

Commentary

Doc Vickerson is characterized as "a fat old man and dirty and unvirtuous" and also as "a gray mass of a man with a gray mass of mustache." Yet he feels that his own life has been misspent and that he has wasted time collecting a scientific museum which no one wants to see. He hopes for better things for his young assistant, who should read not only Gray's *Anatomy,* the Bible, and Shakespeare, but should also attend college before entering medical school. The magnifying glass represents the boy's spirit of investigation, so important in the years that now lie before him.

The first chapter gives the Middle-West setting of the novel and introduces the determined character of Martin Arrowsmith, already absorbed in medical interests.

Though perhaps not a typical doctor of his time, Doc Vickerson is yet able to fire the ambition of his young protege, and to advise him about preparation for the future. The sordidness of the background is typical of Lewis's realistic point of view.

CHAPTER II

I

Summary

The mythical state of Winnemac, bounded by Michigan, Ohio, Illinois, and Indiana, is half Eastern, half Midwestern, with Zenith, its largest city, surrounded by fields of corn and wheat. The University of Winnemac is at Mohalis and has a student body of twelve thousand. Young doctors of philosophy give rapid instruction in courses ranging from Sanskrit to department-store advertising. Graduates of the University, both men and women, are expected to "lead moral lives, play bridge, drive good cars, be enterprising in business, and occasionally to mention books, though they are not expected to have read them."

Commentary

Satire is strong in the description of Winnemac, particularly of its University, which, like the Ford Motor Company, produces standardized products with interchangeable parts. Though they may rattle a little, these products are expected by 1950 to have grown in numbers and influence until they have created a new world civilization: conformist, unimaginative, and dull.

II

Summary

When Martin Arrowsmith enters Winnemac University in 1904 at the age of twenty-one, he is one of only five thousand students. Doc Vickerson is dead and so are Martin's parents, who have left him barely enough money to finance his medical education. His idol is Professor Edwards, known as "Encore," head of the chemistry department. Dr. Norman Brumfit, instructor in English, and Professor Max Gottlieb are also introduced, the latter indirectly through characterization by his colleagues. Martin is impressed by the thought of Gottlieb, different from the others, working alone at night in a laboratory, contemptuous of academic success.

Commentary

Sinclair Lewis is very skillful in presenting Professor Gottlieb through the eyes of his co-workers, emphasizing the wide difference between the real scholar and the conventional ones. Martin's interest in Gottlieb's lonely laboratory work foreshadows events to be developed in later chapters. Gottlieb's poverty and aloofness as well as his devotion to science are in contrast with the easy-going sociability of the other two professors.

III

Summary

Martin's first meeting with Gottlieb is detailed in this section. An academic graduate, who has followed Doc Vickerson's advice to obtain training in the basic sciences, Martin feels somewhat superior to his fellow medics, most of whom have only a high school diploma before entering medical school. He is therefore disappointed and indignant when Gottlieb refuses to accept him as a student of bacteriology, saying that he is too young and that he should come back next year, after he has taken physical chemistry.

Commentary

The character of Gottlieb is further developed as the reader meets him in person instead of through the opinions of others. His warm German accent, his refusal to accept a half-prepared student in whom he is no doubt already interested, and his ascetic mode of living are all skillfully handled to arouse reader interest. Martin, too, is growing mentally and emotionally and is beginning to wonder if Encore Edwards knows everything, after all.

IV

Summary

Two of Martin's fellow students, who are to appear and reappear in later chapters, are introduced here. The Reverend Ira Hinkley is going to be a medical missionary, representing the Sanctification Brotherhood. Clif Clawson, the class jester, irritates Martin. The cadavers on which the medical students work are callously christened "Billy," "Ike," and "the Parson."

Commentary

There is satire in the portrayal of twenty-nine-year-old Ira Hinkley, the "romping optimist who laughed away sin and trouble." Sinclair Lewis, was already planning a criticism of the clergy which was to materialize in *Elmer Gantry* (1927). Both Hinkley and Clawson reappear from time to time as *Arrowsmith* develops.

V

Summary

Although Martin had been a "barb" in college, having belonged to no Greek letter society, he is persuaded in medical school to join Digamma Pi. From this group, though rough and amiable, had come the honor students for the preceding three years. New members in addition to Martin are Ira Hinkley, Angus Duer, Clif Clawson, and "Fatty" Pfaff. Initiation includes smelling asafetida.

Commentary

More of Martin's contemporaries are initiated into Digamma Pi and are to influence his future. Angus Duer is a brilliant and determined student, having been class valedictorian in college. "Fatty" Pfaff, who looks like "a distended hot water bottle," is the butt of many a crude joke.

VI

Summary

Martin's roommates in the down-at-the-heel Digamma Pi residence are Clif Clawson, Fatty Pfaff, and Irving Watters, a serious but dull second-year medic. Martin likes Clif Clawson best, who in spite of his clowning, is more companionable than the others. Martin detests Ira Hinkley, pities Fatty Pfaff, and fears the brilliant Angus Duer, who listens to the jabbering of his fraternity brothers in superior silence.

Commentary

A new member of Digamma Pi, Irving Watters, is introduced and characterized as "smilingly, easily, dependably dull." New light is also thrown on Martin's other roommates, and details to be recalled as the tale progresses are inserted. In preparation for the profession to which he had looked forward all his life, Martin finds "irritation and vacuity as well as supreme wisdom."

CHAPTER III

I

Summary

Two more teachers in the medical school of the University of Winnemac are introduced: Back Bay Bostonian Dr. John A. Robertshaw, professor of physiology, and Dr. Oliver O. Stout, professor of anatomy. Both are erudite but colorless men. Members of Digamma Pi, thirty in number, aid each other in memorizing long anatomical lists of nerves and muscles while devouring their meals.

II

Clif Clawson, always the practical joker, drops a pancreas into the hat of a visiting banker on tour of the University, much to the chagrin of Dr. Stout and the secretary of the medical school. Reverend Ira Hinkley, who witnesses the act, threatens to expose Clawson but is dissuaded by Martin and Angus Duer.

III

Martin's two companions, Clif Clawson and Angus Duer, show him different worlds in the city of Zenith. With Clif, Martin drinks beer and discusses unfavorably various campus practices and personalities. With Angus Duer, Martin attends a concert of classical music and begins to realize his deficiency in knowledge of literature, music, and art.

IV

Madeline Fox, "a handsome, high-colored, high-spirited, opinionated girl whom Martin had known in college," is a graduate student in English, preparing to teach. Martin feels that she possesses the culture which he lacks and that in addition she is "so darn lovely." Their romance is delayed, however, by his intense studying for final examinations.

V

Fatty Pfaff is a special problem to his fraternity brothers because of his inability to remember facts, in spite of frantic coaching until two o'clock in the morning. Finally the president of Digamma Pi stuffs a "crib" in Fatty's pocket, which he stoutly refuses to use but to which he refers in desperation during the exam. He gets through.

VI

Martin's fraternity brothers tire of his critical attitude and his exalted opinion of Gottlieb. Duer sourly reminds him of his lack of knowledge of foreign languages, architecture, important novels, and current events. Martin should "shut up or get out."

VII

Clif Clawson withdraws from Digamma Pi after many clashes with Angus Duer, and Martin also resigns, planning to room with Clif the following autumn. That summer Martin spends with a crew installing telephone lines in Montana. On his return to medical school, he is to realize at last his ambition of working with Gottlieb. He is thinking also of Madeline Fox, Clif Clawson and Angus Duer.

Commentary

This chapter introduces several new characters: Professors Robertshaw and Stout, and the first woman to appear in the story, Madeline Fox. The ways of medical students of the times are reflected and also satirized in the horseplay of Clif Clawson, the cold and superior attitude of Angus Duer, and the condoning of "cribbing" in Fatty Pfaff. Martin is led to realize his own shortcomings through the caustic comments of his contemporaries. The chapter looks forward to two things for Martin: a romance with Madeline Fox and a year under the tutelage of Gottlieb.

CHAPTER IV

I, II, III

Summary

Professor Max Gottlieb infects a guinea pig with anthrax germs before a nervous bacteriology class, too respectful to stand close. He advises his students to be careful about infecting themselves when handling deadly germs and that the most important part of experimentation is not the experiment itself but taking "accurate, quantitative notes" in ink.

Duer observes to a fraternity brother that Gottlieb might have been a first-rate surgeon and made fifty thousand dollars a year instead of four thousand as a laboratory man. Martin Arrowsmith, however, visualizes himself as doing the same experiment.

The guinea pigs die in two days, and the class reassemble for the necropsy. Smears from the lungs, spleen, liver, and kidneys of the animals are made on glass slides and examined under a microscope. The uneasy class members recall nervous rumors of a former student who had died from infection under such circumstances.

IV

Martin, in imitation of Gottlieb, has begun working in the laboratory at night with an enjoyment little short of ecstasy. One evening the young student is invited to share coffee and small, foreign sandwiches with his master at midnight.

Gottlieb talks of the laboratories of London and Sweden and the epidemic in Marseilles as well as of his family: a sick wife, a son, and a daughter, Miriam. He recalls events of thirty years ago, such as his expulsion from Germany for refusing to sing *Die Wacht Am Rhein.* He wonders wryly whether deadly germs should be prevented from killing off at least a part of the human race, thus solving economic questions. The young scientist and the old look at the slides before Martin says goodnight.

Commentary

The personality of Gottlieb shines throughout these pages, the true scientist in a world of froth and fraud. The effect of Gottlieb's teaching, his experiments, and his confidences is to deepen Martin's admiration of the man and his lifetime devotion to the search for truth in the field of Martin's own choice. The guinea pigs and their experimental scientific treatment foreshadows the use of *phage* later on to control a plague in humans.

CHAPTER V

I

Summary

Bacteriology dominates Martin's life now, although he is also studying pathology, hygiene, surgical anatomy, and several other subjects. His roommate, Clif Clawson, though still a joker, supplies cheerfulness, for "The whole of Clif was more than the sum of his various parts." Martin seldom thinks of his former fraternity brothers. He is more interested in rebelling against the cut-and-dried teaching of the professor of *materia medica,* Dr. Lloyd Davidson. Clif becomes impatient with him. For diversion and understanding, Martin returns to Madeline Fox.

II

Madeline encourages Martin to complete his medical courses before deciding exactly what he will do. Her widowed mother, who has come to live with Madeline, supplies a home and a chaperone for her daughter's entertaining, which is on a higher cultural and social level than that to which Martin is accustomed. A rival is Dr. Norman Brumfit, professor of English, who is in favor with Madeline. Martin, however, obtains permission to call on her the following evening.

III

The evening is a disappointment, because Mrs. Fox remains in the room the entire time, and Martin is forced to talk to her instead of to her daughter. In the half-minute when he has Madeline alone, however, Martin manages a goodnight kiss.

IV

A round of parties with Madeline as hostess follows, in which Martin is always a central figure. Even Clif Clawson is dragged in as an extra man. "Martykins" is the pet name bestowed on Arrowsmith, and soon not only Clif but Fatty Pfaff and Irving Watters are using it, to Martin's consternation. Clif, enraged, warns Martin against marrying a girl of Madeline's tastes, who will reduce him to the status of a tonsil-snatcher.

V

Madeline undertakes to improve Arrowsmith by urging him to increase his vocabulary and improve his taste in fiction. She also advises him to omit slang from his speech. He proposes to her one night in her roof garden, after she has brought up the subject of probably having to go home without her Ph.D. They are to be married after he finishes two more years of medicine and two in the hospital.

VI, VII

Mrs. Fox accepts Martin as her future son-in-law, and the three of them attend Methodist Church together. The Reverend Ira Hinkley gloats over Martin's captivity.

Madeline, however, keeps scolding him for feeling superior and objecting to his working with Clif Clawson as a waiter in a Canadian hotel during summer vacation. As a result of her nagging, Martin, after learning that he has been appointed undergraduate assistant to Gottlieb for the coming year, takes off with Clif to the North woods without seeing her again.

Commentary

Martin's first serious love affair develops and almost ends in this chapter. Having outgrown the limitations of Digamma Pi, he with Clif Clawson enjoys more independent living until Martin turns to Madeline Fox for companionship and help. She introduces him to a different world—one of culture, refinement, and gracious living, but she is too eager to change him. He rebels, for he must choose between her and bacteriology. He cannot become a mere money-grubber. His trip to the North woods and a position as waiter in a resort hotel constitute a declaration of independence against conformity. Leading the class in bacteriology and being appointed assistant to Gottlieb open the way for future developments in his career of scientific investigation.

CHAPTER VI

I

Summary

Martin returns from Ontario more in love with Madeline than ever, and they are reëngaged. Twenty minutes later she is sneering at Clif Clawson, at fishing, and at all schoolteachers.

II

The junior year of medicine is "a whirlwind." Martin does his first original research in a manner that evokes praise from the meticulous Gottlieb.

III

Gottlieb sends his assistant to a hospital in Zenith, where he becomes lost and encounters a probationer nurse who is scrubbing the floor. She is Leora Tozer.

Within half an hour the two are well enough acquainted for Martin to plan a dinner date for the evening. They dine together twice in two weeks, and only twice in that time does Martin see Madeline. Leora is never critical or corrective, and Martin is at ease with her. She tells him of her home, the tiny sordid village of Wheatsylvania, North Dakota, and of the Tozer family. Soon Martin is engaged to two girls at once.

IV, V

That evening Clif and Martin visit a tavern together, and under the influence of liquor Martin telephones both Leora and Madeline late at night to meet him the next day at lunch, eleven-forty, at College Square. Both accept. By bringing the two girls together, Martin expects to find out which one loves him. Next morning he wakes sober, "with a crackling skull" and a realization that he is going to face both his fiancées at lunch.

The meal at the Grand Hotel is a painful one. Stylish Madeline patronizes untidy Leora by inquiring about her family, the West, and all the personages of Zenith society whom Leora could not conceivably know and whom Madeline herself knows but little. At last Martin is forced to blurt out the purpose for which he has brought them together—that he is engaged to them both. Madeline springs up, stares at them, and walks away, wordless. Leora has won, and she vows never to give Martin up.

Commentary

"I am stupid and ordinary and she isn't. I simply admire you frightfully...while she has sense enough to make you admire her and tag after her."

This remark made by Leora after Madeline releases her hold on Arrowsmith reveals the diversity of character traits in the two women. One would change and reform the man she marries. The other would submerge her own personality in his.

In this chapter Sinclair Lewis deals briefly with romance, giving it some surprising turns, such as the planned meeting of the two fiancees. His first wife, Grace Hegger Lewis, is thought to be the original of Madeline Fox. Evidently Lewis prefers the permissive type of woman, exemplified by Leora, especially for the wife of a character like Arrowsmith, whose first love is science with everything else in the world secondary.

CHAPTER VII

I, II, III

Summary

Martin's relations with Leora seem calm and serene after his more turbulent connection with Madeline. When Digamma Pi is giving a dance, he and Leora shop together for his clothes, finally deciding on dinner jacket and black waistcoat. When they arrive at the ball, however, many of the men wear white waistcoats and even white gloves. At first Leora has no dancing partners, but after Fatty Pfaff breaks the ice by asking her to dance, she has partners galore. Martin stands and watches her jealously, refusing to ask other girls to dance. She notices his attitude and tells him how much she enjoys dancing and her "dandy partners," promising that she is absolutely his and forbidding him ever to be jealous again. From now on he is her slave.

IV, V

Clif Clawson, too poor to attend the ball, meets Martin and Leora afterwards at the door of the Imperial Cafeteria. Clif is favorably impressed by Leora, even though she seems to look through his boasting. When Martin is snubbed by Angus Duer, he feels that the insult is directed at Leora. Next day, however, Duer apologizes for his conduct, saying that he had had a headache the evening before; he offers to share four tickets for *As It Listeth,* a play with a New York cast, if Leora will bring one of her friends and make a foursome. Leora invites a probationer nurse, Nelly Byers.

VI

Things happen fast after the play, which all four enjoy on different intellectual levels. After Miss Byers goes home by trolley car in order to be in the hospital by a quarter after eleven, the other three linger over beer and Swiss cheese sandwiches. Angus addresses himself to Leora in a way that makes Martin jealous. Arriving at the hospital after hours, Leora is hoisted through a window by the two men. Martin follows to kiss her goodnight, while Angus falls asleep on the stone steps. The night watchman accosts Martin on leaving, and a scuffle ensues, in which Martin barely prevents Angus from stabbing the watchman with a pen knife. The two young men escape through an alley and board the trolley. Next morning Duer is clear-eyed as usual and rebukes Martin for being "stewed" the night before.

Commentary

This important chapter advances the story of the romance between Martin and Leora, at the same time throwing new light on the deep-seated characteristics of Angus Duer. Contrast in the two probationary nurses is obvious, Nelly being punctilious about keeping hospital hours, and Leora being careless. This disregard of convention makes Leora all the more alluring to Martin. Again he is made jealous by Duer's attentions to Leora, conferred in rather condescending style. The suave, city-bred Duer shows a surprising murderous streak in his nature, however, when he loses entire control of himself and tries to kill the night watchman.

Suspense is built up from the beginning of the chapter to its lively end, and more action and less detail are included than in much of Sinclair Lewis's writing. The subject matter is also less technical than usual, there being only a few references to medicine and research. Social affairs, such as the ball and the play, are used as background, reflecting life of the times. Even "white mule" is mentioned casually.

CHAPTER VIII

I, II

Summary

Martin's duties in assisting Max Gottlieb involve sixteen hours a day. Dr. Silva, dean of the medical faculty and devotee of Sir

William Osler, is revered by the young medic, but Dr. Roscoe Geake is hated. Upon leaving the University for the vice-presidency of a powerful medical furniture and instrument company in New Jersey, Dr. Geake offers worldly-wise advice in a farewell address to the students of Winnemac. He stresses the importance of salesmanship in the medical profession and the desirability of accumulating "good hard cash."

III, IV

Leora has been summoned home to North Dakota, perhaps for months, and Martin, sick and lonely, sees her off at the Union Station. With Clif Clawson he develops the habit of getting drunk only to find that when the effect of the liquor wears off, he is even more weary and lonely.

Then comes the Founder's Day dinner at the University. Clif, always the practical joker, invites a bogus professor, introduced as Dr. Benoni Carr, to be the chief speaker. The spurious Dr. Carr becomes drunk and creates a rowdy scene at the dignified banquet. As a result Clif Clawson, knowing that he will be expelled from the University, withdraws of his own accord to become an automobile salesman, and Martin is left more lonely than ever.

Commentary

The loneliness of life at the University with both his closest associates, Leora and Clif, gone is reflected in Martin's conduct and in his attitude toward his work, which remains adequate but not outstanding.

The hoax perpetrated by Clif Clawson on the dignitaries of Winnemac seems a bit incredible. That a man who "had been a 'spieler' in medicine shows, chiropodist, spiritualist medium, esoteric teacher, head of sanitariums for the diversion of nervous women" can hoodwink the authorities into believing him a great pharmacologist is a neat bit of Lewis satire, of the tongue-in-cheek variety.

CHAPTER IX

I

Summary

Clif Clawson, now a successful automobile salesman, drives into Zenith at the dizzying speed of thirty-eight miles an hour. The year is 1908. Noisy as ever but better groomed, he takes Martin to dinner at the Grand Hotel, where they are joined by George F. Babbitt, ten years their senior and now a real estate king. To Martin, poor and shabby, Clif seems like Napoleon and Babbitt another Gladstone.

II

Leora writes that she may not be able to return to Zenith, and Martin is upset and lonely. Gottlieb, who is "jumpy and testy" from working eighteen hours a day, in a rage fires Martin as assistant because of a mistake involving experimentation on rabbits. Martin, half intoxicated, is summoned before Dean Silva, who warns him to turn over a new leaf or face suspension for the rest of the year. Martin refuses to apologize to Gottlieb and is therefore dropped from the University, with six dollars in his pocket.

Martin seeks Clif Clawson, from whom he borrows a hundred dollars to go to Leora. He becomes a hobo, however, and works at odd jobs such as that of dishwasher and soda-clerk, mainly because of mental frustration but partly because of his desire to keep the borrowed money intact for his reunion with Leora. He finally sends her a telegram saying that he will arrive in Wheatsylvania at 2:43 Wednesday.

III

Leora, in a big coonskin coat, is waiting for him in front of the "red box of a station." He promptly tells her that he has come to marry her. She objects that her father will never consent, as he has had no part in the planning. Martin is unfavorably received by Mr. and Mrs. Tozer and Leora's brother, Bert, but in spite of them he manages to elope with her by train the next morning. That afternoon at one they are married in the county seat, Leopolis, by a German Lutheran minister. The whole rampant Tozer family meet the newlyweds at the station upon their return. No one but Leora listens to Martin's remarks that he is a good young man, a wonderful bacteriologist, and able to take care of his wife. In the midst of the argument, Leora coolly lights a cigarette and diverts the attention of her scandalized family to her and away from her husband.

Mr. Tozer mildly orders the family to "stop scrapping," since there is no proof that Martin is an unsuitable husband for Leora, and since he is returning to medical school at once. Leora is to remain with her family until after Martin's graduation and is never to smoke another cigarette. Three days later Martin walks into Dr. Silva's office at Winnemac.

Commentary

Twenty-five dollars a week, plus commissions, was wealth in 1908, and Clif Clawson flourishes it in the face of impecunious and high-minded Martin Arrowsmith. Another go-getter, George F. Babbitt, already familiar from the novel which bears his name, is introduced as the typical big-businessman. Already he is headed toward politics and expects in ten or twelve years to represent the state of Winnemac in Washington, D.C. Lewis through satire brings out the inequity in pay and prominence between hollow men and those of genuine ability and character.

The disagreeable Tozer family is introduced in this chapter: Mr. Tozer, slightly more reasonable than the others; Mrs. Tozer, always whining, and even feigning illness; the fiery, argumentative Bert; and his fiancee, Miss Ada Quist, who "seemed to speak with her pointed nose as much as with her button of a mouth." They are to make matters difficult for Martin but at the same time to push him on through medical school.

Martin's marriage to Leora is set against a background of intolerance. His break with Gottlieb and the University is a device to get him out of Winnemac and into the western wheatfields, where the drab village of Wheatsylvania and the still more drab and hostile Tozer family give him an unfriendly welcome. Mr. Tozer, however, is the first to accept Martin as a son-in-law and to arrange for him to return to Winnemac and finish his medical degree.

CHAPTER X

I, II

Summary

Dr. Silva welcomes Martin back to medical school and congratulates him on his marriage. Leora, permitted to write once a week, tells Martin that she has been dropped from the school of nursing because of absence and of being married. She is secretly studying shorthand and trying to learn typing so that she can earn money as a stenographer. Martin decides to return to Wheatsylvania and demand that his father-in-law support Leora and finance a course in stenography for her while her husband is finishing his degree. After much wrangling, the request is granted, and Martin and Leora leave for Zenith with the promise of seventy dollars a month from the Tozer treasury.

III, IV

Martin finds Leora a room in Zenith nearer Mohalis than her hospital had been. This is their first home. She studies in the Zenith University of Business Administration and Finance. It takes her six months to learn enough stenography to work in an insurance office. At least two nights a week Martin spends with her. Though she knows little of medicine, she understands his philosophy and the basis of his work. She makes him physically comfortable and keeps out of his way while he studies. She gives him security. He has transferred his admiration and loyalty from Gottlieb to Silva.

V

A year and a half whirl by between Martin's marriage and his graduation. Clif Clawson is a buoyant companion until he leaves for New York and a new motor agency. Mr. Tozer becomes more cordial, although he sends irritating fatherly advice with every check.

VI

The seniors are all trying to decide which branch of medicine to pursue after graduation. Should they remain general practitioners or become specialists? Angus Duer chooses surgery, Fatty Pfaff obstetrics. Martin considers first one specialty, then another, before deciding that after his internship is over he will accept Tozer's offer to help him set up office as a country doctor in Wheatsylvania. Angus stands first and Martin seventh in the class. Now he is Martin L. Arrowsmith, M.D., house physician in Zenith General Hospital.

Commentary

Martin's student days are over, and his internship is beginning. His marriage has had a wonderful effect on him, since he has practically quit drinking and finds complete contentment in his relationship with Leora. Yet the thought of Gottlieb and scientific research will occasionally intrude, and he still dreams of a small laboratory of his own. The idealist in him is not entirely subdued.

The first phase of the novel, Martin's schooling, is now complete, and the narrative moves on to his internship. Leora, the ideal wife for a man of Martin's temperament, gives him security and contentment. She assumes her part of their financial burden as well, although she is not well equipped for a career outside the home.

CHAPTER XI

I

Summary

Martin begins his experience as a house physician by treating a factory worker who has been suffocated by smoke in a fire at Boardman Box Factory. The spectacular ride to the scene of disaster in an ambulance and the subsequent treatment of the victim give Martin a feeling of superiority, pushing laboratory and test tubes into the back of his mind.

II

The first year of his internship Martin is thrilled by his battle against fire, flood, and disease. The second year such experiences become routine. He is homesick for the laboratory and "the search for fundamental laws which the scientist...exalts above temporary healing." An evening that he and Leora spend as guests of Dean Silva nearly convinces him that the life of a practitioner is preferable to that of a laboratory man; but a chance meeting with Gottlieb and Leora's unbounded praise of the wretched but great man make Martin wonder again about his choice. In the meantime he finishes his internship and leaves Zenith for Wheatsylvania.

Commentary

His training finished, Martin Arrowsmith, M.D., is now ready to move on to independence and Wheatsylvania, and to become a full-fledged general practitioner. This transitional chapter also brings Gottlieb back into the story, again in contrast with Silva. With almost incredible insight and understanding, Leora instantly realizes Gottlieb's greatness. "He's like a sword—no, he's like a brain walking!" she tells her husband. "I'd black his shoes!"

The rift is not healed at the time, however, and Martin goes his way to become a square peg in a round hole, a practicing physician in Wheatsylvania.

CHAPTER XII

I, II, III

Summary

Dr. Max Gottlieb is a German Jew who has never been interested in practicing medicine but always in laboratory research. He had married the "patient and wordless daughter of a Gentile merchant." He is over-cautious about announcing results of his research, always waiting for definite proof and hating men who rush into publication unprepared. He has been on the faculty of Winnemac for twelve years. Teaching bores him, but he appreciates the excellent facilities for work and some of the brigher students. Poverty keeps him from travel and enjoyment of worldly pleasures.

Gottlieb's family consists of his wife, slow-moving and not well, and three children. Miriam, the youngest, is interested in classical music; her older sister is "nothing in particular"; and the son is wild, with no taste for study.

One of the few students to appreciate the true work of Gottlieb is Martin Arrowsmith. Gottlieb is willing, therefore, to go to great lengths to help Martin with his career. After the break between them, Gottlieb delays appointing a new assistant, hoping that Martin will come back, and is chagrined and grieved when he does not.

IV

Shortly before Gottlieb meets Martin and Leora on the street, his fortune has taken a turn downward. He has offended the authorities at Winnemac by proposing to bring in a research man from Harvard to replace Silva. At a meeting of the Board of Regents the aging scientist is asked to resign. His attempts to find a better position immediately are futile.

In the meantime, Mrs. Gottlieb becomes acutely ill, and Dr. Silva is summoned to treat her ailment, which he diagnoses as probably gastric ulcer. Gottlieb fears that it may be cancer. She is hospitalized for several weeks and improves. Things go from bad to worse for Gottlieb, who is by now reduced to applying for employment to a Chicago teachers' agency. He is insulted by being offered a position as high school teacher of physics and chemistry. A later offer, which he also rejects, is one to teach Practical Hygiene in Edtooth University, which has the biggest gymnasium in the world and a New York Giant for baseball coach.

Commentary

This chapter and the next bring the reader up-to-date about the events surrounding Gottlieb from the time of his break with Arrowsmith until his employment by McGurk Institute. Both are full of irony. Scientists are valued almost as highly in Great Britain as "distillers, cigarette manufacturers, and owners of obscene newspapers," and "catching microbes" is "no work for a tall man at a time when heroes are building bridges, experimenting with

Horseless Carriages, and selling miles of calico and cigars." Such are the values in Sinclair Lewis's America of the early 1900's. Great benefactors of humanity and their works are overlooked.

Gottlieb's nondescript home and family are practically detached from his scientific career. The only satisfactory child is Miriam, the music student. Mrs. Gottlieb is a nonentity, of peasant extraction and tastes. Yet she contributes to her husband's welfare by providing him with a comfortable home background, although she has no conception of the world of science in which he lives.

CHAPTER XIII

I, II

Summary

Gottlieb finally finds employment with Hunziker Pharmaceutical Company, of Pittsburgh, an institution that he has always criticized for doubtful vaccines and money-making addiction. Since he is to be given free range in the laboratory, however, he accepts with joy. Dr. Rouncefield, in his Chicago clinic, chuckles over the change in one whom he considers a "super-highbrow." In Wheatsylvania, North Dakota, young Dr. Arrowsmith protests to Leora that he never believed Gottlieb would fall for "those crooks." Leora insists that there must be a good reason for it. Gottlieb and his family immediately move to Pittsburgh and five thousand a year.

III, IV

The first six months in Pittsburgh proceed well. Not until then does Gottlieb realize that his young technical experts resent his thrusts at commercialism. He also discovers that Hunziker Company is producing and selling unethical products on the side, such as a "cancer remedy" with the value of mud and a complexion cream guaranteed to turn dark skin white.

At this time Gottlieb makes a discovery that is the culmination of twenty years of test tube research. Immediately Dawson

Hunziker tries to force the scientist to produce the antitoxin in large quantities and to market it at once. Gottlieb, wishing for further proof of the serum's efficacy, delays production, to the irritation of Hunziker. In the meantime Mrs. Gottlieb dies; Robert, the son, develops extravagent and dishonest character traits; and the older daughter elopes with a gambler. Gottlieb sits alone, reading the book of Job.

Miriam, however, rises to the occasion. She discontinues her music lessons and takes over the household. Then Gottlieb receives an offer to become chief of the Department of Bacteriology and Immunology of McGurk Institute of Biology, in New York, at a salary of ten thousand a year. This old and reputable firm is on a sound ethical as well as financial basis, with be-whiskered Dr. A. DeWitt Tubbs as director.

Commentary

Throughout his employment by Hunziker, Gottlieb remains steadfast in his convictions, refusing to compromise even for the sake of fame and money. His new position with McGurk is more in keeping with the character of the man. He suffers the afflictions of Job in his family life, but he is never resentful and never gives up his ideals of pure science.

These two chapters (XII and XIII) bring the Gottlieb story up to the time of Arrowsmith's becoming established in Wheatsylvania. There is some parallelism between the careers of the old scientist and the young during this period, both being forced by circumstance into avenues not in line with their more specialized abilities.

CHAPTER XIV

I, II

Summary

The contentious Tozers make life disagreeable for Martin, trying to control his movements in every detail from punctuality at suppertime to the choice of an office location. Always the emphasis is on saving money. Mrs. Tozer would have placed his office in the barn. Bert would have had Martin trundle his luggage from station to house in a wheelbarrow, to save a quarter.

"But a doctor has to keep his dignity," insists Leora, who is always on her husband's side. When she demands that her father lend Martin and her a thousand dollars to use as they see fit, there is at first an outcry of protest, but Leora wins the skirmish. After two weeks of waiting for the Norbloms to decide whether or not they will vacate an apartment suited to the needs of the young physician, he finds a solution in renting a shack for fifteen dollars a month from "Wise the Polack." For the first time in his life, Martin has an office of his own, and with Leora he is proud and content.

Martin's first patient is a chronic complainer, Miss Agnes Ingleblad.

Commentary

In great detail Sinclair Lewis characterizes the members of the Tozer family and their neighbors, with all their narrowness, bickering, and absurdities of reasoning. Leora stands out in relief against such a background. Only she can win any favors from her family.

The narrative progresses as Arrowsmith opens his office and begins his actual practice of medicine.

CHAPTER XV

I, II, III

Summary

Martin orders his office equipment from the New Idea Instrument and Furniture Company, whose vice-president is his former preceptor, Dr. Roscoe Geake. He rejects the recommended Tonsillectomy Outfit but includes a steel stand, a sterilizer, flasks, test tubes, and a combined examining chair and operating table. A new plate glass sign with gold lettering reads: "M. Arrowsmith, M.D." He and Leora are in ecstasies. His own surgical case, including dental forceps, he had brought from Zenith. His first office patient is Nils Krag, with an ulcerated tooth that is extracted.

A five-year-old Ford is acquired for making country calls. Leora also learns to drive it, but it is Martin who becomes the demon driver of the village.

Pete Yesta, the local druggist, is antagonized when Martin criticizes his inaccuracy in filling prescriptions. Thereafter Martin has to prepare his own medicines or obtain them from St. Paul.

IV, V

After a wild race in his Ford, first to a farmhouse where a child is dying of diphtheria and then to Leopolis, twenty-four miles away, for antitoxin, Dr. Arrowsmith returns to his first desperately ill patient just before she expires. Shocked by the turn of events, he considers giving up practice of medicine, but Leora comforts and encourages him. He then visits Dr. Adam Winter, the seventy-year-old physician of Leopolis, to discuss the outcome of the case. Dr. Winter turns out to be a fee-splitter, but he exonerates Martin in the death of the child through an article in the local newspaper. The child's parents, at first antagonistic, become Martin's staunch supporters and patients.

Commentary

Two physicians are satirized in this chapter: Dr. Roscoe Geake, who reappears as vice-president of an important instrument company, and Dr. Adam Winter of Leopolis, who proposes fee-splitting to Martin.

Dramatic are the events surrounding the death of the child, Mary Novak – the wild rush for antitoxin, the arrival too late, and the final admission by her parents that they had waited too long before calling the doctor. Martin's whole-souled absorption now is saving lives, and laboratory work is pushed aside for the time being. Always the comforting figure of Leora is in the background, offsetting the effects of less agreeable people and events.

CHAPTER XVI

I, II, III

Summary

A year and a half pass while Dr. Arrowsmith is becoming established in Wheatsylvania. Occasional lapses into drinking and all-night poker playing tarnish his reputation to some extent, but in general his practice improves. He and Leora now have their own home.

Not wishing to become fixed in "a routine of prescriptions and bandaging," Martin seeks a stimulant in Dr. Hesselink, of Groningen. The forty-year-old physician advises studying at home, increasing his vocabulary, and freeing it of slang. Martin begins reading aloud to Leora – Conrad, European history, etc.

IV, V

Gustaf Sondelius, a Swede by birth and a German by education, is to come to lecture in Minneapolis. Since medical school days Martin has admired this man and his war on disease. Leora, after four months of pregnancy, loses her child, and she and Martin realize that there can never be another.

Commentary

Martin, though less distinguished than the town barber, less prosperous than the carpenter, and less interesting than the garageman, is nevertheless known as "reliable, skillful, and honest." This bit of irony is matched by the fact that the garageman, the bootlegger, and the undertaker are considered more desirable associates than is the United Brethren minister.

The realization that other things count as well as knowledge in one's special field is brought out in Martin's frantic attempts at self-education. He is to do much studying of this type in years to come.

The fantastic character of Sondelius is introduced in this chapter. He is to be of importance later on. The loss of their unborn child only brings Martin and Leora closer together.

CHAPTER XVII

I, II

Summary

Dr. and Mrs. Coughlin, of Leopolis, take a tour in their three-year-old Maxwell car and eventually visit Dr. and Mrs. Tromp, in another North Dakota town. The two doctors discuss collections, treatment of certain ailments, and other doctors, including Dr. Winter and a brainy but brash young physician, Arrowsmith. They regret that he has no church affiliation, since it is good for business, and deplore his fondness for the bottle. Bert Tozer hears of Dr. Coughlin's disapproval of Martin and urges him to cut out poker and booze. Martin feels resentful that the whole world is watching him.

III, IV, V

Martin is successful in perfecting a vaccine to control blackleg in cattle. The veterinarian of the county denounces him for intruding; the physicians hint that treatment of cattle is beneath the dignity of the medical profession. Martin, however, has once more tasted laboratory life.

Leora urges Martin to go alone to Minneapolis to hear Sondelius lecture. Described as a "Newfoundland dog of a man," Sondelius sways his audience with his anecdotes of the achievements of great men in the medical profession. After the lecture Martin lingers to invite the speaker to join him in a beer garden. From now on Sondelius, not Gottlieb or Silva, is Martin's idol.

Commentary

Sinclair Lewis is giving Arrowsmith some first-hand experience in the practice of medicine before returning him to the laboratory, his original love. The plague among cattle furnishes the opportunity for Martin's renewed interest in research. The fantastic character of Sondelius, who is to play almost a major role in the book later on, is introduced, and his relation with Martin cemented here.

CHAPTER XVIII

I

Summary

Martin becomes a volunteer assistant to the Superintendent of Health, Dr. Woestijne. He denounces accumulation of dirt and trash in yards and streets and criticizes the school board for lack of building ventilation and instruction in toothbrushing. He traces the origin of the typhoid epidemic to a seamstress, who is a carrier, and launches a campaign for smallpox vaccination. When all but the first case turn out to be chicken pox, Martin is the butt of ridicule and feels that he is "licked." He and Leora decide to move on to a larger place.

II, III

Through the influence of Sondelius and upon the recommendation of Dr. Silva and Professor Gottlieb, Martin obtains an assistantship in Nautilus, Iowa, not far from Zenith, under Dr. Almus Pickerbaugh, Director of Public Health. His salary is to be twenty-five hundred dollars a year. He will be epidemiologist, bacteriologist, manager of clerks and nurses, and inspector of sanitation. He and Leora board the train, after apologetic and regretful farewells by such neighbors as Pete Yesta, Dr. Hesselink, and Henry Novak.

Commentary

The Wheatsylvania episode is now finished, and Martin and Leora move out of North Dakota to Iowa and a different life. The fact that Martin's tormentors regret his going is proof that they appreciate him more than he thinks. A new phase of the story, the Nautilus one, is about to begin.

CHAPTER XIX

I

Summary

Nautilus, a town of seventy thousand, is to Zenith what Zenith is to Chicago. A few score people are wealthy, the rest mostly industrial workers. Mugford Christian College has never bothered to teach biology, much less the theory of evolution.

II, III

Martin's director is Dr. Almus Pickerbaugh, head of the Department of Public Health. Forty-eight years old, he looks like Theodore Roosevelt and makes as much as possible of the resemblance. In poetic ability he likens himself to Longfellow. His health jingles are particulary trite and boring to Martin, though Leora considers them "cute." The Pickerbaugh family, in addition to the husband and father, consists of the mother and eight "bounding daughters," the oldest being nineteen-year-old Orchid, who likes men.

Dr. Pickerbaugh is involved in so many extracurricular activities that the list makes Martin's head swim. The young physician's life is supposed to follow the same pattern. Leora comments that he has a job that will take twenty-eight hours a day, with the rest of the time for research, barring interruptions.

IV

During an interminable evening at the Pickerbaugh home, when Martin and Leora are overfed, and worn to a frazzle with after-dinner games, Orchid takes advantage of the opportunity to become quite familiar with the young doctor. Leora is jealous and on the way home reminds him that he is hers and that she will tolerate no trespassers. Over coffee at an all-night lunch wagon Martin hears the workingman's evaluation of Pickerbaugh, which is favorable.

Commentary

Sinclair Lewis is never nearer Dickens than in this chapter. The very name of Pickerbaugh, with its irony, recalls Micawber, Pecksniff, Chuzzlewit, and a dozen others. The extreme extrovert qualities of the man and the multitude of activities, serious and inconsequential, in which he is involved identify him with the American go-getters, however, already depicted in *Babbitt*. As a result of the impossible load of duties assigned to him, Martin is almost ready to grab Leora and to take the next train out of town. His better judgment, however, causes him to remain and to try the position for a while, in spite of his disappointment in regard to laboratory work.

CHAPTER XX

I, II

Summary

Martin and Leora are courted by "Nice Society" in Nautilus. Dr. Irving Watters, formerly of Digamma Pi, is now a leading physician, and he and his wife, the near-wealthy daughter of the manufacturer of Daisy Manure Spreader, undertake to initiate Martin and Leora into the social life of the community. Mrs. Watters firmly but politely tries to correct the "barbarism of the Arrowsmiths" by rebuking Martin's language, Leora's smoking, and both their bridge games. Watters is still as enthusiastic but dull as he had been as a student.

III, IV

Martin's first lecture is received with "most enthusiastic applause." His only critic is Leora, who is keen-sighted enough to realize that he may have his head turned by too much attention. They come near quarreling on the subject, and on that of Orchid Pickerbaugh. Leora admits, however, that her Sandy has to stumble every so often and that he learns from his mistakes.

The afternoon of the Pickerbaugh's snow picnic Leora goes coasting with the school physician, a bachelor, and Martin with Orchid, making matters worse.

Commentary

"Nice Society" is satirized in this chapter, along with social and professional climbing and temporary fame. Leora's criticism, though caustic, has the effect of keeping Martin, who thinks rather well of himself, on the conservative track. The chapter advances the narrative of the years in Nautilus and links Martin's present life with his past by reintroducing Irving Watters, now a physician with three years of experience.

CHAPTER XXI

I, II, III

Summary

Nautilus, under the leadership of Pickerbaugh, is among the first American communities to develop the *weeks* habit: Swat the Fly Week, Gladhand Week, Better Babies Week, and a host of others. Martin balks at More Babies Week, as he believes in population control.

Irving Watters and other such physicians attack Pickerbaugh, fearing that if his health campaigns are too successful, their income will be reduced. When Martin suggests to his superior that more could be accomplished by pasteurizing all milk and by burning down disease-infected tenements than by parades and slogans, Pickerbaugh declines to follow such procedures for fear of offending people.

Martin's laboratory, though well equipped and lighted, is little satisfaction to him because of constant interruptions by trivial matters.

IV

The Pickerbaugh daughters, notably Orchid, furnish some of the interruptions in Martin's laboratory; Orchid does her painting and lettering there. Leora can always tell when he has spent an afternoon with Orchid. When in the summer of 1914 Leora goes to visit her family for two weeks, Martin finds solace in Orchid's company. Once he kisses her, and after that she becomes a nuisance, telephoning him every few hours. He realizes that her intelligence is too low for her to be admitted even to the mediocre local college. Martin is happy when Leora returns.

Commentary

The American way of life, with its clean-up campaigns, its high-powered boosters, its money-grabbing, and its deficiencies beneath the surface is the target for Sinclair Lewis's satire again in this chapter. Nautilus has more special weeks than the year contains. The character of Orchid, healthy and handsome but brainless, is notable only because of her impact on Martin. That Martin's luke-warm affair with her should be his first and practically his only extra-marital venture is also ironic. The narrative has now covered the period from 1897 to the summer of 1914, just before the outbreak of World War I.

CHAPTER XXII

I, II

Summary

Pickerbaugh is nominated for Congress by the Republican party and leaves Martin in charge of the Department while the candidate is out campaigning. One of Martin's first acts as director is to quarantine Klopchuk's diary and one of the milkers with a chronic sore throat, found to be streptococcus. An epidemic is threatened. A specialist from Chicago is called in, and he agrees with Arrowsmith. Irving Watters, Klopchuk's physician, considers Martin an alarmist.

III, IV, V

The Arrowsmiths become close friends of the Clay Tredgolds, "on the loftiest plains of Nautilus society." Martin gives an imitation of Pickerbaugh, and Leora is proud of him. Martin and Leora are henceforth accepted by the "Smart Set" of Nautilus, including the Schlemihls and the Mugfords, even higher in the social scale than the Tredgolds. Soon the young doctor and his wife are members of an exclusive country club, whose members are very rich.

Leora belongs to a bridge club and goes to the movies alone. Yet her one expressed aspiration is to go to France. Martin promises that they will do so some day.

Martin is to be the next director of the Department. Pickerbaugh observes that the young man lacks only one quality: pulling together with others.

Commentary

The rapid rise of the Arrowsmiths in the social world is paralleled by Martin's rise to the directorship of the Department of Health. "I won't *lay* down!" he exclaims ungrammatically. "I'll fight!"

Leora, by her refusal to imitate her fashion-plate associates in dress, remains the sloppy but faithful wife, always putting her husband's interests above her own.

The wealthy come in for their share of satire. Motoring, drinking, dancing, and cards are their chief diversions. They are most interested in cars, shower baths, stylish clothing, "impersonally decorated" houses, and trips to New York or Paris. Today such things are called status symbols.

CHAPTER XXIII

I, II, III, IV

Summary

The Health Fair is highly successful until the last day, which brings both rain and fire. Pickerbaugh, with rare efficiency and presence of mind, takes over and prevents people from being trampled. Now he is more than a local hero, and his election to Congress is assured. Soon he leaves for Washington with his family, and Martin is now appointed acting Director of Health. His youth and the opposition of Jordan prevent a permanent appointment. Martin's salary is thirty-five hundred a year instead of four thousand.

Pickerbaugh's leaving for Washington is celebrated lavishly. The mayor speaks, the band plays, and the station is jammed with thousands as the train bearing the waving Congressman-elect puffs out of sight. Martin never sees Orchid again.

Commentary

The rise of a politican opens the way to promotion for Martin. Yet jealousy and opposition prevent him from obtaining all that he deserves. This is realism. So are some of the fantastic happenings at the Health Fair.

CHAPTER XXIV

I, II, III

Summary

With his assistant, young Rufus Ockford, from Winnemac, Martin tries to clean up Nautilus and free it from rats, fleas, and disease. He has time again for laboratory work and is happy. Then a storm breaks.

Martin and Ockford head a gang which invade and tear down unsanitary tenement houses belonging to Mrs. McCandless. At first the reaction of the influential Tredgold set is favorable, but later their attitude changes when Martin refuses to leave his laboratory to join in a Saturday night frolic.

Opposition to Martin develops on all sides at once. He blames himself again, feeling that he is a failure. His salary is cut again to the point that he is practically forced to resign or starve. He gets in touch with Angus Duer in Chicago.

IV, V, and VI

Angus Duer, now a highly successful surgeon with Rouncefield Clinic in Chicago, offers Martin a salary of twenty-five hundred dollars a year instead of four thousand, previously mentioned. Martin accepts. Pickerbaugh writes a letter from Washington indicating that he is disappointed in Arrowsmith. Martin vows that he is "licked" again and that he is through from now on with everything but moneymaking.

Commentary

Again the conscientious but hard-headed Arrowsmith is the victim of forces too strong for him and is practically driven from his position in Nautilus. Refusing to become a playboy with the Tredgold set, he loses their friendship and influence. The mayor, the Parents' and Teachers' Association, and all the fashionable churches turn against him. Klopchuk and F. X. Jordan label him as crooked. Even Pickerbaugh repudiates him.

Once more Sinclair Lewis uses Martin's unpopularity as a seeker of truth as a device for bringing about a change of scene, this time from Nautilus to Chicago.

CHAPTER XXV

I, II, III

Summary

Martin's year at Rouncefield Clinic is spent among "Men of measured merriment," to use a phrase coined by Gottlieb. He is "a faithful mechanic—in a most clean and brisk and visionless medical factory."

He and Leora, however, gain in knowledge and experience. They read novels and history, and they travel; they attend plays; they meet important people at dinners given by the Rouncefields and the Duers; and Leora begins lessons in French. Yet Martin realizes the hollowness of it all, especially when he is urged by Duer to turn his laboratory experimentation into something practical. He does so, publishes an article in the *Journal of Infectious Diseases,* and attracts the attention of Max Gottlieb, who extends an invitation to join him in McGurk Institute, New York.

Commentary

Again Martin fails to find the true spirit of science in a new and coveted position. Again the upper social strata are satirized in the wives of Rouncefield, Duer, and the suave set which forms their circle. Martin is now ready to move on to a broader and more colorful world in New York, taking Leora with him. She has tried to keep pace with him in cultural improvement, though she is never really tidy in personal appearance. Their marriage relation is deepened by the experiences they share.

CHAPTER XXVI

I, II, III

Summary

After a year in the Chicago Loop, Martin is not overwhelmed by New York, although he does admire the Woolworth Tower. He finds that Max Gottlieb has aged in the last five years, though Gottlieb is still as demanding as ever. He advises Martin to study mathematics in order to be able to prove his own experiments. In half an hour the two are arguing as fiercely as in the old days.

Martin is at last permitted to concentrate on laboratory work, with no additional duties. He is elated. So is Leora for him.

IV

The year is 1916. Europe is at war. Social life for Martin and Leora begins in New York by their being invited to scientific dinners, first by Ross McGurk, founder of the Institute, and his wife, Capitola, and later by Dr. Rippleton Holabird, head of the Department of Physiology, and Mrs. Holabird. The only jarring note in Martin's life is Terry Wickett, the "boy chemist" as he styles himself, who is irritating, rude, and iconoclastic, but devoted to the search for scientific truth.

Mrs. Holabird helps Leora find a three-room flat near Gramercy Park, where Martin rashly hopes that they will stay for fifty years.

Commentary

Gottlieb's hatred of pseudo-scientific impostors and his creed that the real scientist accepts no half-truths is again emphasized in this chapter. Martin's prayer of the scientist is one passage in the book often quoted:

> God give me unclouded eyes and freedom from haste. God give me a quiet and relentless anger against all pretense and all pretentious work and all work left slack and unfinished. God give me restlessness whereby I may neither sleep nor accept praise until my observed results equal my calculated results or in pious glee I discover and assault my error. God give me the strength not to trust in God!

The disagreeable but genuine character of Dr. Terry Wickett appears for the first time in this chapter. He is to be of considerable importance later on.

CHAPTER XXVII

I, II, III

Summary

Slow and tedious experiments are not so to Martin. Tubbs gives the young man vague encouragement. Gottlieb asks him discomforting questions. For all his fumbling, Martin has "wide-ranging...unself-dramatizing curiosity," which drives him on.

Mrs. Ross McGurk, whose given name is Capitola, is a great uplifter. Her husband has bought the Institute to keep her out of his other business interests, including shipping and mining. Descended from California railroad men and possessing a Yale degree and unlimited cash, McGurk admires and even becomes friends with the cynical Gottlieb. Capitola has no share in this friendship. Gottlieb refuses to open his laboratory to guests at one of her intellectual dinner parties. Her husband forbids her to "get funny with Max," but she is still uncontrollable, especially in regard to the monthly scientific dinners.

The first of these functions to be attended by Martin and Leora has as an honor guest Major-General Sir Isaac Mallard, a London surgeon. Terry Wickett is rude to the chief guest, and he, Martin, and Leora leave early because of the shallowness of the small talk.

IV, V

Holabird is too fond of self-praise, and Martin becomes disgusted. He finds that his colleagues are divided into several factions, the ruling caste being Tubbs, Holabird, and Tubbs's secretary, Pearl Robbins. Allied with Gottlieb are Martin, Wickett, and Dr. Nicholas Yeo, with Dr. Sholtheis leaning in their direction. Dr. William Smith keeps to himself.

Martin is amazed and hurt when Gottlieb and Wickett insist that he needs to study mathematics and physical chemistry as a background for his laboratory work. He bores Leora until two in the morning, however, with algebra, trigonometry, analytic geometry, and differential calculus. He also reads the classics of physical science. So absorbed is he in study that he hardly notices when America enters World War I in 1917.

VI, VII

Dr. Tubbs offers the services of the Institute to the War Department, and all the doctors are made officers. Only one, Terry Wickett, goes to France. The others are uncomfortable in their uniforms and in doubt about when to salute. Otherwise the pattern of their lives is not greatly changed.

Gottlieb, however, as a German Jew, is a target for insulting remarks and even suspicion. His son, Robert, joins the United States army to fight against his cousins, who are Germans. Gottlieb's strong accent and his expressions, such as *Auf Wiedersehen,* bring criticism, and the old man is very sad.

The McGurk staff members do more than wear uniforms, however. They prepare sera, invent electrified wire entanglements, and work on poison gas. Martin is conscious of Gottlieb's suffering and tries to console the old man, though kindness to the unfortunate is not one of Martin's qualities. His research wipes everything else from his mind and makes him turn his war work over to others.

Commentary

This chapter brings the narrative up to the year 1917 and America's entrance into World War I. The narrow-mindedness and intolerance of people in the grip of war hysteria is brought to light in realistic fashion in the callous treatment of Gottlieb. There is irony, too, in the switch by McGurk Institute from concentration on means of preserving and prolonging life to means of destroying it. To Martin, although assigned research connected with the war effort, the whole episode is but an interruption of his own line of scientific investigation.

CHAPTER XXVIII

I, II, III

Summary

Martin notices that one of his carefully nurtured laboratory cultures has "committed suicide." He becomes vastly curious as to the cause. He is sure that the culture has staph in it. All one night he makes tests and at seven in the morning calls the hospital for more pus from the same carbuncle. Finding that the carbuncle is now healed, he can obtain no more of the same material. He rushes home to tell Leora of his discovery, only to find her gone in search of him. Visions of having arrived after years of stumbling flit through his brain.

For a week he hardly eats or sleeps, so intense is his concentration on his experiment. Gottlieb is critical, as usual, but makes some suggestions that help Martin confirm his findings of the X Principle. The reaction of close application and loss of sleep is too much for the young physician, however, and he drifts toward neurasthenia. He becomes extremely nervous, noises annoy him, and he is the victim of fears and delusions. Four days spent tramping through the Vermont hills build up enough reserve energy to support him for a while after he goes back to his experiment.

Commentary

Sinclair Lewis's own fears and phobias are thought to be reflected in this chapter, for example the fears connected with a railway journey. Martin still finds a balance wheel in the mature Gottlieb, who asks just the right questions and uses just the right psychology to keep his younger colleague on the right track. Leora is, as always, a sanctuary for her overwrought husband. The big break in Martin's career is now in the offing.

CHAPTER XXIX

Summary

After six weeks of intensive work with the X Principle, Martin learns that the Director of the Institute knows of the unusual results. McGurk summons the young scientist, congratulates him, and offers to create a Department of Microbic Pathology with Martin at the head. The yearly salary is to be ten thousand dollars. Both McGurk and Holabird wish to share Martin's success with him. He is urged to publish his results immediately but demurs and stalls for time to accumulate further proof. Leora is impressed with the prospect of more money and a higher standard of living and for once encourages her husband to accept the terms that are offered him. They are extravagantly entertained by Capitola McGurk at one of her dinners, where the honor guest is the sister of a countess and where Martin has to listen to chitchat that bores him intensely.

Bad news is in the offing, however. Next morning Gottlieb breaks the news that D'Herelle, of the Pasteur Institute, has just published a report identical with that of Martin's X Principle, called "bacteriophage." At first Martin is upset and disappointed, but after he realizes that he will not have to be a department head and publish reports before he is ready, he is consoled. He will try to corroborate the findings of the Frenchman and will rename the X Principle *phage*. Again he will be free to work in his laboratory without fanfare. If Leora is disappointed, she keeps her feelings to herself—mostly.

Commentary

The transitory quality of fame and fortune is emphasized in this chapter. This time Martin is cheated out of the credit for his amazing discovery, not by Tubbs and Holabird, who would force him to share the credit with them, but by a high-type rival scientist who had announced his findings just a little too early. Martin greatly admires D'Hérelle's report and is free from jealousy of a scientist greater than himself. With his solitary and retiring disposition, he is somewhat relieved that he can now go back to his laboratory in peace, although he is sorry for Leora's disappointment.

CHAPTER XXX

I, II, III

Summary

A year passes. Terry Wickett returns after the Armistice, and Martin keeps up his laboratory work, studying mathematics and physical chemistry and reading books written in French and German on the side. Tubbs resigns as Director of the Institute to double his salary by working for a millionaire named Minnigen and his League of Cultural Agencies. Instantly there are diverse applications for the position of Director, Rippleton Holabird being an insistent one. To his own surprise as well as that of others, however, Gottlieb is asked to accept the position. He does so, and within a month the Institute becomes a shambles.

IV, V

The unworldly and scholarly Gottlieb plans to give only one hour daily to the business, devoting the remainder of his time to research. He appoints Dr. Aaron Sholtheis, the epidemiologist, as his assistant. Both the Director and his assistant are besieged by advocates of unquestionable cures they claim to have discovered. Miss Pearl Robbins, the secretary, is the actual Director, and the Institute "reeled with intrigue." In the midst of the turmoil appears Gustaf Sondelius, back from a study of sleeping sickness in Africa. He joins the staff, and he and Martin recall with pleasure their earlier meeting in Minneapolis. Sondelius becomes a great admirer of Martin's discoveries, and the two become collaborators in investigation of a possible cure for bubonic plague, known as the Black Death. Gottlieb is commendatory of the experiment, but Wickett remains cool. Martin and the flamboyant Sondelius form a team of which Martin is the leading spirit.

Commentary

Sinclair Lewis brings back most of the characters introduced in the earlier part of the book, making this the best plotted of his novels. The sensational Sondelius is reintroduced, this time as Martin's follower, not his leader. The narrative sweeps on toward the best and most exciting portion of the book, the use of *phage* in fighting the plague in St. Hubert.

CHAPTER XXXI

I, II, III

Summary

From China the bubonic plague is brought to the West Indies, by way of Marseilles and other European ports. Rats from the infected *Pendown Castle* escape in St. Hubert, and the first victim dies of plague. This small tropical city of a hundred thousand inhabitants is a British possession, the governor being Colonel Sir Robert Fairlamb. Next in social prominence is Sir Robert's critic, Hon. Cecil Eric George Twyford. Kellett the Red Leg, advocate of economy, has dismissed the official rat-catcher of St. Hubert, much to the disapproval of his political enemy, George William Vertigan. Dr. Inchcape Jones thinks that infectious diseases carried by rats can not exist in St. Hubert. Dr. Stokes, an American physician, thinks otherwise, but even when there is a death from the plague, Dr. Jones considers it an isolated case and insists there will be no more. There are more immediately.

Blackwater, the port of St. Hubert, maintains a bar and restaurant known as the Ice House, where homesick rum swizzlers meet. George William Vertigan, a jolly and regular customer, dies of plague two days after a visit there. Panic envelops St. Hubert as the epidemic spreads, although there is no quarantine. Sir Robert Fairlamb tries to reassure the people that there is no danger, but Dr. Stokes of St. Swithin's secretly writes to Dr. Max Gottlieb, Director of McGurk Institute, in New York.

Commentary

A complete change of scene and a new cast of characters are features in this chapter, half a dozen new people being introduced. There is much local color as background for the action, for West Indies scenery is exotic. Descriptions of the disease itself are detailed, horrifying, and no doubt accurate. Years later Albert Camus, French Nobel Prize winner of 1957, was to build a whole novel, *La Peste,* around a similar scourge in Oran. Whether Camus had read Lewis is a matter for speculation. The most exciting and interesting part of *Arrowsmith* begins with this chapter, for all its sometimes revolting realism.

CHAPTER XXXII

I, II, III, IV, V

Summary

Dr. Gottlieb has already heard of the plague in St. Hubert, for Ross McGurk's world-wide means of transportation and communication keeps the Institute better informed than are the residents of Blackwater itself. It is rumored that Arrowsmith of McGurk may have something to eradicate the plague. Martin is summoned and asked if he will go to St. Hubert and experiment with the *phage* on half the patients and keep the others as controls. Martin agrees. Sondelius is to go along for publicity and to see that the Institute receives proper credit, though he is not to participate in the experimentation. Martin is to find if possible a district comparatively untouched by the plague and should there have test cases, one half injected with *phage* and the other half untreated. In the badly afflicted districts he may give the *phage* to everyone. If results are favorable, that part of the experiment will be secondary proof. In the meantime the Surgeon General, Dr. Inchcape Jones, cables that no help is needed. Sondelius considers himself the official rat-killer and is enthusiastic about the job.

When Martin breaks the news of his departure to Leora, she insists on going along, since she has no life of her own outside of her husband and his work. He will need her help, she argues, for she has helped him before in the laboratory, and in addition he may become ill. She wins her point.

Gottlieb warns Martin not to let a kind heart spoil his experiment in St. Hubert, for it is necessary to think of generations to come as well as of men now dying. Terry Wickett admonishes Martin to keep his *phage* notes complete and up-to-date, in ink.

Before the McGurk Commission sails, the island of St. Hubert is under quarantine. Dr. Inchcape Jones has declared that people may come in, but that none may go out. Martin buys a supply of tropical-weight clothing to take along, in addition to his syringes and his ampules of *phage*.

VI, VII, VIII, IX

Martin, Leora, and Sondelius sail one winter morning on the steamer *St. Buryan,* of the McGurk Line. Only Terry Wickett sees them off. It is the first sea voyage for the Arrowsmiths, though Sondelius is a globetrotter. Gottlieb arrives at the dock too late to find them at the rail. He is disappointed.

Martin and Leora are seasick off Cape Hatteras, but enthusiastic about their voyage. Leora has brought a West Indian guide book and reads it avidly. Sondelius is all over the ship, striking up acquaintance with all kinds of people. A Miss Gwilliam, from New Jersey, makes him conscious of his lack of culture and refinement, but not for long. Martin becomes conscious of how much he has neglected Leora and promises to do better. So great is her absorption in him that she has never felt neglected and makes light of his attempts to apologize. He promises her that on their return from St. Hubert they will take the coveted trip abroad, so that she may see England and Italy, and most of all, France. She is ecstatic over the prospect of "going places." In their close little stateroom she tries to make him as comfortable as possible and adores him more than ever.

Commentary

The representatives of McGurk Institute are drawn into the narrative again and are now on the way to the West Indies, Martin of course being in the lead. To Ross McGurk the expedition furnishes an opportunity for the Institute to acquire world-wide fame; to Gottlieb, Martin, and Sondelius it is an attempt to acquire further scientific knowledge, at the same time saving lives. The whole-souled absorption of Leora in her husband is again brought into the narrative, this time leading her into grave danger with him. She admits being lazy, useless, and ignorant except for the protection and love she gives him. Sondelius, once Martin's leader, is now cast in a subordinate though important role. He has qualities which Martin lacks, and the two complement each other. The episode builds up to its highest point, the actual fight against the plague.

CHAPTER XXXIII

I, II, III

Summary

None of the tourists aboard the *St. Buryan* had known of the quarantine before leaving New York. Now they realize that once they go ashore at St. Hubert they will be prisoners there for the duration of the epidemic.

Martin begins to wish that he had forcibly left Leora behind and tries to convince her that she should stay on the ship, but to no avail. Upon landing, the travelers are met by Dr. Stokes, the port doctor having died a few days before. Many of the servants are also dead, and hotel living is by no means comfortable. Martin hopes that Leora does not see a wagon piled with a dozen dead bodies which they encounter on the street. The spirits of Sondelius, however, are still high, and he dons a dressing gown of surah silk last worn on the East Coast of Africa. Inchcape Jones has scarcely finished his call on the newcomers when the new arrivals have another caller, the Rev. Ira Hinkley, now at work saving souls and incidentally bodies in the plague-stricken area.

IV, V, VI

In the afternoon Inchcape Jones takes the Commission to his home, Penrith Lodge, in the hills behind Blackwater. On the way they pass a schoolhouse turned into a pesthouse, with a hundred cases of plague within. Martin establishes a small laboratory with the equipment he has brought. His first caller is a Negro doctor, Oliver Marchand, M.D., who is familiar with Martin's experiments and is doing all he can to fight the plague.

While Martin is establishing his laboratory, Sondelius launches his anti-rat campaign, terrifying the Board of Health and dragging people of all occupations from their work to follow out his instructions.

Commentary

Again Sinclair Lewis unifies the novel by bringing in still another member of Digamma Pi after years of absence from the story – Ira Hinkley. Ebullient and obnoxious as ever, Hinkley is still detested by Martin Arrowsmith.

All the sordid happenings of the chapter are set against a background of natural beauty of the tropical West Indies. Only one new character is introduced, the Negro doctor, Oliver Marchand, progressive, well-read, efficient, and dedicated to his profession.

CHAPTER XXXIV

I, II, III

Summary

Inchcape Jones drives Martin to the village of Carib, worse stricken than Blackwater. The rat-fleas have infected the ground squirrels, and Carib has death in every house. The horrors that Martin beholds almost turn him from his determination to experiment as Gottlieb had ordered. Since Inchcape Jones does not understand the need for experimentation, Martin calls on the Governor, Colonel Sir Robert Fairlamb.

Sir Robert and Lady Fairlamb are at dinner when Martin arrives. At first Sir Robert listens politely but later loses his temper and tells Martin that he will do all that is possible to prevent "Yankee vivisectionists" from experimenting in his domain.

Thanks to Sondelius, however, Martin is able to present his case before a special Board composed of the Governor, Inchcape Jones, Sondelius, Oliver Marchand, and a few others, while Leora listens to her husband's address from the back of the room. All except Stokes and Marchand are against Martin and his experimentation, considering him a fanatic.

Into the midst of the discussion plunges Ira Hinkley, missionary of the Sanctification Brotherhood. He brings up the information that both Arrowsmith and Gottlieb were dismissed from Winnemac and labels them lunatics. Cecil Twyford, of St. Swithin's Parish, arrives too late for the special Board meeting but offers the help of St. Swithin's in obtaining what the Board refused.

Four days later Ira Hinkley is dead.

IV, V, VI, VII

In Carib, Martin has a chance to give the *phage* to the population as a whole, and the plague begins to decrease. Now he hopes to try test conditions and soon after that to be on the way home with Leora. It is necessary to burn the village in order to rid it of the infection. Sondelius catches the plague and dies, having refused from the first to be inoculated with the serum.

Panic is increasing in Blackwater, for the people now believe that Martin is withholding from them the drug that can save their lives. Sir Robert Fairlamb is a "blundering hero"; Stokes attends his stricken patients, with only three hours sleep at night; Leora helps Martin prepare *phage* at Penrith Lodge; and Inchcape Jones goes mad and commits suicide after an abortive attempt to escape from the island.

With the appointment of Stokes in Jones's place, Martin, as medical officer in complete charge of St. Swithin's Parish, now has his experiment made possible. He leaves Leora at Penrith Lodge with maids and a soldier butler and takes up his residence temporarily in the Twyford home, to be nearer his great experiment.

Frangipani Court, abode of the Twyford family, is occupied by Cecil Twyford himself, his mother, and five sons. His wife has been dead ten years. A guest in the home is Joyce Lanyon, widow of the wealthy Roger Lanyon, of New York. She has come to the Indies to see her plantations and has been trapped by the plague. So striking is her physical resemblance to Martin that he feels she must be his sister, his twin. She offers to help him with nursing or cooking, and he accepts her offer, all the time intending to send for Leora as soon as possible.

Commentary

Martin's success as a scientist is saddened by the death of Sondelius, an event foreshadowed by his refusal to be inoculated with the *phage* until the natives have been served. The demented suicide of Inchcape Jones shows how humans may crack up under pressure. New characters are introduced in the chapter: the Twyford family and the widowed Joyce Lanyon, for whom Martin feels a strange attraction, although he is still faithful to Leora. The West Indies episode is now at its height, and the reader looks forward to the success of the experiment and the return of Martin and the others to New York.

CHAPTER XXXV

I, II, III

Summary

The plague has only begun to invade St. Swithin's when Martin divides the population into two equal parts, injecting one half with the plague *phage* and leaving the other half unprotected. The unphaged half has far more victims than the other, and Martin is elated. Cecil Twyford risks his life nursing his servants, and Joyce Lanyon takes over the cooking, bedmaking, and other maid's duties.

The bond of resemblance as brother and sister is tightened as Martin and Joyce work together, although he struggles against his liking for her. After trying for two hours to reach Leora by telephone, he gives up, assured that within three or four days he can go for her and bring her to St. Swithin's.

IV, V, VI, VII, VIII

Left practically alone in the big house, Leora is lonely and sleepless. She has forgotten to take another injection of the *phage,* as Martin had asked her to do. News comes that Oliver Marchand, the Negro physician on whom she is dependent for medical care, is dead. The butler leaves to go to his sister, ill of the plague. Leora goes to Martin's laboratory, picks up one of his half-smoked cigarettes, and lights it.

A maid had knocked over a test tube on the cigarette, and it contained enough plague germs to kill a regiment. Two nights later, Leora becomes violently ill and dies alone in her bedroom, calling for Sandy until she falls into the coma preceding death.

Joyce Lanyon, like Sondelius, tries to persuade Martin to give the *phage* to everyone. He explains Leora to Joyce before going to Penrith Lodge for his wife, only to find her stiff and lifeless. He goes to pieces and begins drinking heavily. He does not care whether he lives or dies and sits talking to Leora and Sondelius, Hinkley, Marchand, Inchcape Jones, and others among the dead. For some time he does not see Joyce Lanyon, but one day she appears, straightens his room, and offers him friendship, which he rejects and goes back to rigid observation of his St. Swithin experiment.

The epidemic subsides, and six months after Martin's coming, the quarantine is lifted. The first steamer leaves, with Joyce Lanyon aboard. Martin has asked to come to see her in New York. All the while he is mourning for Leora.

Martin becomes a dignitary because of his success with the *phage.* No one heeds a Scotch doctor who hints that plagues sometimes run their course without *phage*. A letter from Holabird brings news to Martin that Gottlieb, in poor health, has resigned as Director of McGurk Institute and that Holabird is now Acting Director. Martin is offered a promotion as head of a new department. He feels that he has been a traitor to Gottlieb and all that the old scientist represents. In spite of an elaborate farewell dinner the evening before his sailing, Martin dreads explaining matters to Gottlieb and Terry Wickett.

Commentary

Death removes two important characters from the novel: Leora and Sondelius. Lewis probably gets rid of them so as to give Martin more freedom of action upon his return to New York. He is eager to get back to his lab and "start all over again." His friendship with Joyce Lanyon foreshadows events to come. The excitement and horror of the West Indian part of the story end with this chapter, and another change of scene is expected. The beauty of the landscape is brought out in sharp contrast to the intensity of human suffering the chapter contains. An example of local color used as contrast follows:

> From a hilltop they swung down a curving road to a beach where the high surf boomed in limestone caves. It seemed impossible that this joyous shore could be threatened by plague, the slimy creature of dark alleys. (Chapter XXXIV)

CHAPTER XXXVI

I, II, III

Summary

Martin returns to New York on the *St. Buryan,* where he encounters Miss Gwilliam again, returning from a winter in Trinidad and Caracas. She receives short answers when she inquires about Sondelius and Leora and draws the conclusion that he is stupid and not very successful. Other shipboard acquaintances think that he is in love. Martin is eager to get back to his test tubes but is afraid of criticism because he believes that his experiment has too many loopholes. He decides to take his tables to a biometrician and to be governed by expert advice as to what to publish. For the first time in weeks he sleeps without terror.

IV, V, VI, VII

To the astonishment of his fellow passengers, Martin is greeted at the pier by reporters, from whom he is rescued by Rippleton Holabird, now full Director of the Institute. Terry Wickett gives Martin a delayed welcome and brings the news that Gottlieb is now on pension. With Leora, Sondelius, and Gottlieb gone, Martin now has only Terry as a kindred spirit, and the two promise to stick together.

Martin is received with much acclaim by the Institute, the newspapers, the Public Health service, and even Congressman Almus Pickerbaugh. He refuses all invitations to speak, however. Foreign Men of Measured Merriment are brought in to see him. He is made head of the new Department of Microbiology at twice his old salary. He calls on Gottlieb, who does not recognize him. He closes the flat where he and Leora lived and takes a room at a hotel. Then he takes his figures to Raymond Pearl, the biometrician, who decides that the results of Carib village should be questioned, as the epidemic may have passed its peak before inoculation began. Holabird advises Martin to issue an ambiguous summary. Martin is furious. He knows that Holabird has barely skimmed the report and is far from understanding it. Terry Wickett encourages Martin to remain with the Institute a while, as there is more math and chemistry to learn, and Martin needs a laboratory.

Commentary

The shallowness of Holabird and the genuine scholarship of Wickett, concealed under a rough exterior, are again emphasized in this chapter. Terry's reference to his shack in the woods of Vermont is an example of foreshadowing. Satire of the Institute and its high officials is prominent, also, for Martin is expected to rush into print and popularity before the results of his experiment can be thoroughly checked. Even Wickett, however, admits that except for being "a dirty, lying, social-climbing, sneaking, power-grabbing hypocrite" Holabird is all right.

CHAPTER XXXVII

I, II, III, IV, V, VI

Summary

Martin is lonely in New York after his return from the West Indies, having been reduced from Dr. Arrowsmith to a man with no one to talk to. He finds a companion in Joyce Lanyon, who knows how to make men talk. He visits her in her palatial home, to the disapproval of Latham Ireland, a well-dressed lawyer, also an admirer of Joyce. The luxury surrounding her, as well as her wealthy friends and lavish entertaining, hold Martin in awe.

Joyce becomes an arranger, a sponsor of causes. The part of her life which she feels to have been most useful, however, is that in which she played the part of an almshouse cook. She teaches Martin bridge and plays tennis with him. They are married with pomp and ceremony the next January in St. George's Church. Terry Wickett refuses to act as best man. For three months they travel in Europe, Martin having for the first time the opportunity to observe the great laboratories of London, Paris, and Copenhagen. He is happy except for dreadful seconds when Leora floats between them, she who never realized her aspiration to see France.

Martin, with his limited knowledge of women, has much to learn from Joyce, who besides being his wife is a wealthy and socially prominent woman. He superficially masters her way of life, but when he has a clerk telephone her that he is busy in the laboratory and cannot meet her at dinner, she is enraged.

Commentary

Sinclair Lewis has been building up to this second marriage of Arrowsmith for several chapters. The wealthy and socially important Joyce is a far cry from the simple, careless Leora of Wheatsylvania, North Dakota. The ways of the rich are satirized through the characters of Joyce and her friends: their week-end parties, their display of luxury, their insistence on their own accepted codes of behavior, and their shallowness beneath the surface. In contrast again is Terry Wickett, with whom Martin is no longer free to escape to the Vermont hills. Martin is torn between devotion to his work and loyalty to his wife.

CHAPTER XXXVIII

I, II, III

Summary

Director Rippleton Holabird, jealous of Martin's newfound magnificence, which includes a limousine and a chauffeur, retaliates by shifting Martin's work from *phage* to influenza vaccine. After months of half-hearted experimentation, Martin tells his superior that Rockefeller investigators have found the cause of the flu and that he is going back to his first love, *phage*. His report stirs the laboratory world.

Then Martin joins Terry Wickett in experiments with quinine derivatives. They spend a winter together at Birdies' Rest, Terry's crude laboratory in the Vermont hills. When they return to New York, their request for money and monkeys to use in their work is granted. When they supposedly have a cure for pneumonia, however, they refuse to publish it prematurely. Terry argues with Holabird and is discharged, and Martin plans also to return to Vermont. Joyce is quite unhappy over her husband's conduct and reminds him that she is expecting a baby. He asks if she is willing to spend part of the year in a little house near the woodland laboratory, but she does not consent.

Commentary

The rift between Martin and his second wife is deepening, for he is too serious-minded to accept her way of life. He turns from one extreme to the other in clinging to his partnership with Terry Wickett. Satire of high society continues in this chapter. The superficiality of Holabird is again brought to attention. So is the principle of exploitation of scientific knowledge for the sake of money and fame.

CHAPTER XXXIX

I

Summary

Clif Clawson, Martin's college roommate, reappears in the story after an absence of many years. Clif is as boisterous as in the days of Digamma Pi. At forty he is not only a boor but a swindler. In spite of his bad manners and worse morals, he persuades Martin to invite him to the Arrowsmith home to meet Joyce. Martin reluctantly does so, and Joyce arranges a dinner for only the three of them. Martin tries to explain Clif to her, but that is impossible. She is shocked and bored with his company, excusing herself early. Clawson is offended, and Martin feels that he has lost the best friend he ever had. The two never meet again.

II, III, IV, V, VI

The son of Martin and Joyce, John Arrowsmith, is named for two of his grandfathers. Three months after his birth Joyce is more brisk than ever in her social life and advancement of pet schemes. As a surprise for Martin she creates for him the best bacteriological laboratory he has ever seen, in order to keep him near her while he works. The Rolls-Royce set can also come and observe the great scientist in his laboratory once a week. It is hard to explain to Joyce why sightseers bother him so. Joyce's friends speculate on why she married Martin when she might have had her choice of any number of "well-bred, agreeable, intelligent chaps" more like her first husband.

Joyce's busyness gets on Martin's nerves, but he rejoices in little John. Still he thinks of Leora and her quiet understanding. In the early winter he joins Terry Wickett for a week at Birdies' Rest. The two again agree that they have to stick together.

Commentary

The way in which Clif Clawson has degenerated during the fourteen years since he and Martin last met is another satiric thrust at the go-getter. An overdrawn character, Clawson is still an American type. The Rolls-Royce set, the social upper crust who consider watching Martin work in his laboratory as "diversion in an exhausted world," also, comes in for more barbs. Martin is drifting away from Joyce and her world toward Terry Wickett and his Vermont retreat.

CHAPTER XL

I, II, III, IV

Summary

Rippleton Holabird plans to leave McGurk Institute and help Tubbs guide the League of Cultural Agencies. He offers Martin the position of Assistant Director, soon to become full Director. Joyce is elated with the prospect. They talk the matter over at length, but before morning he moves out of the house and into a cheap hotel, refusing to answer Joyce's telephone call. Next day he catches a train for Vermont and joins Terry "for keeps."

The harsh life of Birdies' Rest is in contrast to the luxury to which Martin has been accustomed. He becomes adjusted to it, however, and is soon engrossed in experimentation with quinine derivatives. His work draws ahead of Terry's. His mathematics and physical chemistry are now as sound as and his imagination more swift than that of his companion. Terry plans to bring in a few more scientists, making a total of eight.

Joyce arrives one day, ready to make peace and to build a house across the lake. When he objects to her bringing people to intrude on his privacy, she says that he is becoming a fanatic and regretfully leaves him. She will probably divorce him and marry Latham Ireland.

Dr. Aaron Sholtheis becomes Director of McGurk Institute; Dr. Angus Duer is Head of Duer Clinic, Chicago; Bert Tozer is still attending midweek prayer meeting in Wheatsylvania, North Dakota; and Max Gottlieb sits "unmoving and alone" in his little room above the city street. Martin and Terry are discussing their new quinine experiments as the novel closes.

Commentary

The ending of *Arrowsmith* is considered less satisfactory than earlier portions of the book. Yet Lewis disposed of practically every important character mentioned, from the members of Digamma Pi to the doctors and scientists of the New York and Chicago clinics. Martin's refusal to compromise his ideals for the sake of wealth and popularity is consistent throughout the novel, giving him the rare attributes of the true scientist.

CRITICAL ANALYSIS

THEME, PLOT, AND STRUCTURE

The *theme* of *Arrowsmith* is devotion to work as typified by Martin's absorption in pure science.

The *plot* of *Arrowsmith*, though somewhat rambling, is the best organized of all the Lewis novels. S. N. Grebstein, in *Sinclair Lewis* (1962), comments that the book's narrative component is superior to that of *Main Street* and *Babbitt,* because the story moves beyond conflicts and centers upon the doctor's war with death. "This grappling with the universal is a rare thing in his [Lewis's] work," according to Professor Grebstein, and "*Arrowsmith* demonstrates more of Lewis the philosopher than any other novel."

Arrowsmith is divided into forty chapters, each subdivided into shorter sections headed by Roman numerals. The book is therefore well adapted for "pick up" reading, since each short unit is complete in itself, at the same time advancing the action and illuminating the background of the novel as a whole. In *structure* the book contains eight principal episodes:

1. Martin's training as a physician-scientist and his marriage to Leora (Chapters I-XI)

2. His experiences as a country doctor in Wheatsylvania (Chapters XII-XXVIII)

3. The years in Nautilus (Chapters XIX-XXIV)

4. Experience in Rouncefield Clinic (Chapter XXV)

5. With McGurk Institute, in New York (Chapters XXVI-XXX)

6. The West Indian adventure (Chapters XXXI-XXXV)

7. Return to New York and marriage to Joyce (Chapters XXXVI-XXXIX)

8. Decision to join Wickett in Vermont (Chapter XL)

Each major episode is almost a complete story in itself, although linked to the whole by the growth and development of the central character. Other characters are important as their lives are intertwined with his. Suspense is maintained throughout the novel, although the ending is rather a letdown after the excitement of the fight against disease in the West Indies.

TECHNIQUE OF TELLING, STYLE, SETTING

The story is told in the third person, the central figure being Martin Arrowsmith, though Gottlieb occasionally takes the center of the stage. The narrative moves for the most part in a straight line chronologically, with few flashbacks but many changes of scene. The characters are the most lifelike that Lewis ever created, especially Martin, Gottlieb, and Leora. The Nobel Prize was awarded because Lewis was "significantly and typically American in his vision, humor, and creation of typical characters." Sometimes the humor of *Arrowsmith* is off-beat, like the macabre pranks played by the medical students on their classmates and others.

Most of the characters introduced early in the book reappear or are at least referred to years later, lending unity to the plot. Examples are the members of Digamma Pi, the Tozers, and Pickerbaugh. Character development and growth are apparent especially in Arrowsmith and Wickett, whose traits are deepened and emphasized with the passing years. In like manner, Clawson and Hinkley degenerate as they grow more mature. There is little change in

Leora or Gottlieb. Romantic love is subordinated to quest for truth. Various social strata are introduced and satirized, from the shoddy farm and village characters of Wheatsylvania to the Rolls-Royce set of New York City. Singled out for special criticism is the Nautilus group, especially the Pickerbaugh family and Irving Watters.

Lewis's *style,* though not of highest literary quality, is yet vivid and readable. He has a tendency toward long sentences, probably in part a result of his wide reading of the nineteenth-century English and American novelists. Dorothy Thompson praised his use of verbs. She also commented that he put far more of himself into *Arrowsmith* than any other book. Lewis uses dialogue sparingly and background liberally, with figures of speech which make his sentences more graphic. The device of breaking each chapter into several divisions keeps the material from becoming too involved and stimulates reader interest.

The *setting* of *Arrowsmith* is American, except for the plague episode in British territory, the West Indies. From Elk Mills to Winnemac, from Zenith to Wheatsylvania, from Nautilus to New York the scene shifts, each time portraying accurately and realistically a certain phase of life in the United States. Words that appeal to the senses—words of color, sound, shape, and motion, and even smell and taste—are used to make the effect more vivid.

SATIRE, REALISM, LOCAL COLOR

Satire holds persons, modes of living, or institutions up to ridicule with the intention of making people laugh so that a change or reform can be brought about. *Arrowsmith* is full of satire of the various strata of society familiar to Sinclair Lewis. Always a radical, always probing the wound instead of applying the plaster, he holds up to ridicule the social climbing, the dollar chasing, and the dishonest motives behind many so-called success stories of the first half of the twentieth century. Each group of characters is subjected to criticism: the students and faculty of Winnemac; the cross-grained and penny-pinching Tozers; the impossible Pickerbaugh family and Irving Watters; the sham and pretense behind the Hunziker procedures; and the hollowness and jealousy among most of the higher-ups at McGurk. Only a few characters, notably Gottlieb and Leora, escape this scathing scrutiny. Even Martin receives a little of it.

The background comes in for its share of analysis. Wheatsylvania, surrounded by a beautiful landscape, is a sore spot on the map. The West Indies, for all their exotic setting, are the scene of death and destruction, with plague-ridden rats peeking from beneath the cargoes being landed on the dock. Hunziker Pharmaceutical Company carries on illicit moneymaking on the side, though outwardly progressive and humanitarian. So pointed was Lewis's criticism that, like Dickens, he sometimes attracted public attention to existing evils.

Akin to satire is *realism,* a term in literary criticism marked by fidelity to actual facts of life, usually the seamy side, with little or no "dressing up" (romanticism). Always a realist, Sinclair Lewis did not try to "gild refined gold" or to "paint the lily."* His pictures of small, sordid American towns as well as those of the larger cities are accurate but unflattering. The Nobel Prize, according to the official citation, was awarded Lewis for his "powerful and vivid art and description and his ability to use wit and humor in the creation of original characters." Like William Dean Howells, he could take the commonplace in American life and make it literary material. Like Edith Wharton, he is also a novelist of manners. The surface detail of America he observed under a magnifying glass: speech, dwellings, marks of social status, pressures, idiosyncrasies, even the plush interiors of the high-priced automobiles of the era. As Lewis was preceded by Emerson, Thoreau, Whitman, and Mark Twain, all of whom railed against mass culture and fixed ideas, so was he succeeded by John P. Marquand, author of *H. M. Pulham, Esq.* and other novels satirizing the mores of later decades in America. Of the two novelists, however, Lewis is by far the greater.

S. N. Grebstein prophesies that Lewis will eventually approxi-

*Shakespeare: *King John,* IV-ii-11,12

mate in American literature the position held by Dickens in England. Both authors discredit the imitativeness and conventionality of other novelists of their own times and reject the theory of "sweetness and light" in literature. Both could seek out the sore spot but left it to others to find a cure. Neither accepted the theory that mankind is in the clutch of circumstances but believed that the individual should be strong enough to overcome odds and fight off pressures. Both criticized manners, morals, and institutions, painting them with all their defects rather than with a glow of unreality, and both could hold the reader spellbound with the leisurely telling of an entertaining story. E. M. Forster likened Lewis to a cameraman, a "photographic realist." Even so was Dickens in his England of an earlier date.

Arrowsmith is rich in *local color,* for Sinclair Lewis saw nature as well as human nature with that same photographic eye. He had a flair for detail that accompanied close observation and keen awareness of all going on around him. This acuteness of senses is not unusual in poets and novelists. Wordsworth had it. Edna Ferber, in *A Kind of Magic*, asserts that she does. Aldous Huxley tried to cultivate it with the use of drugs.

Such *minutiae* as Sinclair Lewis includes make the reader almost hear and see the North Dakota farmlands, the lush but infected St. Hubert, and the clang and clamor of the great cities. Not only details of scenery but those of customs, speech, and personal appearance provide a background for the action. The laboratories in which Martin worked are brought close to the reader; so are the interiors of certain rooms, such as the hall where Capitola McGurk entertained with scientific dinners, as well as the interior of the home in which Martin met Joyce Lanyon, that of the Twyfords at St. Swithin in the West Indies. The reader feels that he has actually seen the places and people that Lewis describes. Local color provides details of scenery, customs, appearance, speech, and human relations.

CHARACTERS IN ARROWSMITH

MAJOR

Martin Arrowsmith

From the time he was fourteen years old, Martin Arrowsmith was preparing for his career as a scientist in the field of medicine. Nothing distracted him more than temporarily from the work he had chosen above all others. While his contemporaries were engaged in money-grabbing, status seeking, and worldly diversions, he remained faithful to his ideals of honesty and the search for truth. Because of this uncompromising attitude, he lost several opportunities for promotion and increased popularity.

Steps in his career included his training in Winnemac, his internship immediately following, his practice as a country doctor in Wheatsylvania, his experiences under Pickerbaugh at Nautilus, his work at Rouncefield Clinic, and finally his position in McGurk Institute, reaching a high point with his fight against the plague in the West Indies. Each stage broadened and strengthened his scientific knowledge and experience, and the disillusionments along the way only served to enhance his radical tendencies and to drive him nearer his final goal, pure research, "far from the madding crowd."* He had sampled several areas of the medical field and found laboratory work most to his liking. He had had two wives of different background and temperament and had moved in various strata of the social world, from life in a crude country village to that of the smart set in New York City. He read and studied in fields other than medicine, including literature, art, foreign languages, and various branches of mathematics.

Yet he decided to shun the so-called civilized world with all its fripperies and to go into semi-seclusion with Terry Wickett in Vermont rather than to continue as the husband of a wealthy New York socialite. Off-beat, radical, yet devoted to his chosen field and untiring in his search for truth, Martin Arrowsmith is one of Lewis's finest creations, reflecting many characteristics of the author himself.

*Gray's *Elegy Written in a Country Churchyard*

Max Gottlieb

Against a background of graft and social climbing and insincerity, the figure of Dr. Max Gottlieb stands out as a pure scientist and a seeker of truth. Lewis modeled him after Jacques Loeb, a prominent United States scientist of the time, born in Germany. Some critics find Gottlieb the novel's most memorable character. Professor Grebstein considers Gottlieb "the kind of man who carries civilization on his shoulders," adding that Gottlieb is "a pessimist who voices his doubts . . . of man's superiority to animals, yet his own genius advances progress and proves man's superiority."

Not a person to cater to public opinion or to his superiors in office, Gottlieb naturally makes enemies. His rift with Martin, caused by a trivial incident, lasts for several years. All the while Gottlieb is changing positions. His home background is adequate but rather stark. Two of his three children are disappointing. He finally sinks into senility before Martin returns from St. Hubert and never comprehends the story of the *phage*. Sympathetic interpretation like that in the case of Gottlieb is rare in Sinclair Lewis, who is cynical toward most of his creations.

MINOR BUT IMPORTANT CHARACTERS

Sondelius

This colorful Swede, the great fighter of plagues, is Sinclair Lewis's own creation, having no prototype as so many of his characters do. It is notable that *Arrowsmith* was not mentioned when Lewis received the Nobel Prize at Stockholm, perhaps because Sondelius did not give a flattering picture of the Swedish scientist. Impulsive, energetic, and hard-drinking, he nevertheless inspired Martin in the early stages of his career and became his servant later on. With reckless disregard of his own health, Sondelius refused to be inoculated with the *phage* until all the islanders were similarly protected. Consequently he had no protection when the plague struck him and perished on the island of St. Hubert. Although his knowledge of medicine is more superficial than Martin's, he is a good mixer, a sincere and enthusiastic worker, and with his extrovert qualities a foil for the studious and withdrawing Martin. Sondelius was a favorite of Lewis himself.

Terry Wickett

In the last third of *Arrowsmith,* Terry Wickett is introduced as an annoying but excellent chemist under Gottlieb in McGurk Institute. "Red-headed, rough-faced, and wiry," he jars Martin Arrowsmith in the beginning with his "rude and slangy" talk, his dissatisfaction with superiors and with the way the Institute is run, and his critical attitude toward Martin himself. Later Gottlieb, Wickett, and Dr. Nicholas Yeo form a faction with which Martin becomes allied. As Angus Duer had earlier made Martin aware of his ignorance of languages, literature, art and music, so did Gottlieb and Wickett cause him to study mathematics, including trigonometry, analytic geometry, and calculus. He also reads the classics of physical science. During World War I Terry joins the artillery and sails for France.

It is not until after the Armistice that Terry returns and that he and Martin are again in conflict, this time over the *phage*. Martin's return home from St. Hubert, however, brings the two together again, and old enmities are forgotten as Martin joins Terry at Birdies' Rest to spend fourteen hours a day in laboratory research, leaving the comforts and wealth of civilized society "to scorn delights and live laborious days."* Thus the thorough scientist, Terry Wickett, finds independence and maturity with his kindred spirit, Martin Arrowsmith.

Pickerbaugh

Dr. Almas Pickerbaugh, Director of Public Health in Nautilus, Iowa, is a caricature of the medical world as Babbitt is of the business world. Preposterous and exuberant, he considers himself just a little below Tennyson as a versifier and a duplicate of Theodore Roosevelt in appearance. His outrageous health jingles are widely copied and repeated, for example:

> You can't get health
> By a pussyfoot stealth,
> So let's every health-booster
> Crow just like a rooster.

Yet Pickerbaugh would make clean the outside of the cup in Nautilus, while unsanitary conditions persisted beneath the surface, for fear of making enemies. Martin saw through this situation at once. More Pickerbaugh satire is concerned with his overwhelming election to Congress and his triumphal exit from Nautilus, accompanied by his wife and eight daughters.

*Milton: *Lycidas,* line 72

MINOR CHARACTERS

The Tozer Family

Exclusive of Leora, the Tozers, of Wheatsylvania, North Dakota, were a disagreeable lot. They were well-to-do for rural people, for Mr. Tozer could afford to send seventy dollars a month to Leora after her return to Zenith with her husband, equivalent to two or three times that sum in purchasing power today. Mr. Tozer, a little more reasonable than his wife and son, Bert, was the first of the family to recognize Martin as a member of the family and to realize that Leora had not made such a bad choice. Mrs. Tozer and her son were alike when it came to pinching pennies. Miss Ada Quist, Bert's fiancée, whom he postponed marrying indefinitely, is a caricature with her meddling and her impecunious ways. All were critical of Martin and wished to control his activities and way of living. Without the help of Leora he could not have held out against them. They are the narrow-minded, small-town type that Lewis often satirized.

Members of Digamma Pi

Several members of the fraternity group with which Martin was identified at Winnemac appear and reappear during the story, giving the plot unity.

Clif Clawson

One of these members is Clif Clawson, an exaggerated character who is a practical joker, a windbag, and a noisy disturber of peace. Yet he furnishes relief as a roommate for the serious Martin, who regards Clif as his best friend. Years later, when Clif is forty, he calls on Martin in New York and boasts about his dishonest schemes for moneymaking and his brushes with the law. Joyce is unfavorably impressed by Clif, as Martin knew she would be, and it is really she who breaks up the friendship between the two men. They had grown apart, however, to such an extent that the old camaraderie was no longer possible. Clif is a satire on the business go-getter who will use any tactics, fair or foul, in dollar chasing.

Angus Duer

Another member of Digamma Pi, Angus Duer is hard and keen, as the name implies. At the top of his class both in college and medical school, he is soon head of Rouncefield Clinic, in Chicago, where everything is cold efficiency for financial gain. He is satirized along with Clawson for his moneymaking tendencies.

The Reverend Ira Hinkley

Older than the other members of Digamma Pi, but bent on becoming a medical missionary of the Sanctification Brotherhood, Ira Hinkley realizes his ambition in the West Indies and dies of the plague. Obnoxious to Martin in college and in later life, Hinkley is a forerunner of Elmer Gantry, who is to appear two years later (in 1927) in the book which bears his name. Through such characters Lewis satirized the churches of his time.

Irving Watters

One year ahead of Martin in medical school, Irving Watters appears as a prominent practicing physician in Nautilus, and it is he with his wife who introduces Martin and Leora into "Nice Society." Watters is just as dull as ever and splits with Martin because the latter insists on sanitary measures that would interfere with business.

WOMEN CHARACTERS

Leora Tozer Arrowsmith

Only three women characters of any consequence appear in *Arrowsmith:* Madeline Fox, Leora, and Joyce. Madeline and Joyce both reflect the characteristics of Lewis's first wife, Grace Hegger Lewis. Leora is probably modeled after Paul de Kruif's idea of his own wife, although a woman novelist, Edith Summers, claimed to be the original of Leora.

Dorothy Thompson considered Leora the most life-like character in all the Lewis gallery, doubting if even her creator realized "how truly her life fulfills the longing of the real woman." When Leora's baby is born dead and she realizes that she can never have another, continues Miss Thompson, she does not despair but becomes more and more absorbed in her husband, not much caring whether she has children or not. Mark Schorer agrees with this estimate of Leora, considering her the most realized figure in all the novels. A few dissenters consider her lazy, careless, and slightly stupid. Yet she never missed a chance to aid her husband, whether by earning a living as a secretary, assisting him in his laboratory work, making him comfortable and keeping in the background when he was studying, or by accompanying him to the plague-stricken West Indies, where she was to meet her own death. It is one of life's ironies that her desire to visit France was never realized. Another is that her husband, within a year or two after her death, married a woman as different from her as one human can be from another.

Madeline Fox

Arrowsmith learned about women from his first love, Madeline Fox. She is the upper middle-class university student, preparing to teach English, who, once Martin is engaged to her, undertakes at once to improve him. Her constant criticism of his slang, his manners, and his way of life becomes tiresome, although he feels that much of it is justified and admits that he needs such help.

Madeline is eager for a husband but wants one whom she can mold to her own liking. Clif Clawson, in spite of his boorishness, realizes that if Martin marries her he will never rise above the level of a "tonsil-snatcher." Madeline is the first of several critics, however, who prod Martin into self-improvement through further study and cultured pursuits, Gottlieb and Terry Wickett being among the number.

Joyce Lanyon Arrowsmith

More sophisticated than Madeline and of higher social and financial standing is Joyce Lanyon, Arrowsmith's second wife. The way in which she wins his esteem recalls the role of Kate Hardcastle in *She Stoops to Conquer*. Joyce in a gingham dress cooking and cleaning in the West Indies is a different Joyce from the fashionable widow who is a leader in the Rolls-Royce set. Her possessiveness and her desire to exhibit Martin and his talents in time become overwhelming, and he goes from one extreme to another in practically abandoning civilization for a chance to pursue his laboratory work in peace.

STUDY QUESTIONS

1. Trace the activities of each of the following members of Digamma Pi throughout the novel, including their influence on the career of Martin Arrowsmith and upon the development of the plot: Ira Hinkley, Clif Clawson, Angus Duer, Irving Watters.

2. Mention five doctors who strongly influence the career of Arrowsmith and explain why each one is important in the story.

3. Compare and contrast the characters of Arrowsmith's two wives, Leora and Joyce. Include their background, social and financial status, appearance, and influence on their husband's career.

4. Compare and contrast the characters of Gottlieb and Sondelius. Include nationality, physical appearance, knowledge of medical science, popular appeal, and the part each plays in the novel as a whole.

5. In what ways do the novels of Sinclair Lewis resemble those of Dickens? Of Mark Twain? Include purpose, development of plot and character, realism, and social criticism of the times in which each author lived.

6. In what ways may *Arrowsmith* be considered a satire? Give concrete examples.

7. Show how each stage of Arrowsmith's progress is reflected in his life and work. Include Wheatsylvania, Nautilus, Chicago, New York, and the West Indies.

8. Would you have the book end differently? If so, why and how?

9. Explain what is meant by *local color*. Comment on several examples from the novel.

10. What to you are the points of highest interest in the narrative? Mention several, and explain your choice.

TOPICS FOR THEMES OR DISCUSSION

1. *Arrowsmith* as it reflects the life and personality of the author.
2. Realism in nature and human nature as found in *Arrowsmith.*
3. American life of the first quarter of the twentieth century as depicted in the novel.
4. The use of satire as an urge for reform (Critical Analysis).
5. The women characters as a reflection of the times (Characters).
6. Medical training and practice in the first quarter of the twentieth century as revealed in *Arrowsmith.*
7. Clif Clawson as a satire on the businessman.
8. Ira Hinkley as a satire on the clergy.
9. Local color and its reflection of human behavior in each of the divisions of *Arrowsmith.*
10. The theme of devotion to work and search for truth as exemplified in Arrowsmith and Gottlieb.

SIX BOOKS ABOUT SINCLAIR LEWIS

Grebstein, Sheldon N. *Sinclair Lewis.* New Haven, Connecticut: Twayne Publishers, Inc., 1962.

Lewis, Grace Hegger. *With Love from Gracie: Sinclair Lewis, 1912-1925.* New York: Harcourt Brace and Company, 1955.

Schorer, Mark. *Sinclair Lewis, an American Life*. New York: McGraw-Hill, 1961.

Schorer, Mark. *Sinclair Lewis* (a collection of critical essays). Englewood Cliffs, New Jersey: Prentice-Hall, Inc., 1962.

Sheean, Vincent. *Dorothy and Red* (Lewis's marriage to Dorothy Thompson). Boston: Houghton Mifflin Company, 1963.

Smith, Harrison. *From Main Street to Stockholm: Letters of Sinclair Lewis, 1919-1930)*. New York: Harcourt Brace and Company, 1952.

A DOZEN OTHER BOOKS BY SINCLAIR LEWIS

Main Street (1920): Carol Kennicott's rebellion against the mores of Gopher Prairie, Minnesota.

Babbitt (1922): the story of a "Tired Business Man."

Mantrap (1926): a novel based on a vacation trip in northern Canada.

Elmer Gantry (1927): a satire on religious sects and personalities of the 1920's.

The Man Who Knew Coolidge (1928): the story of a conformist.

Dodsworth (1929): Lewis's second best novel, with a self-made millionaire as the hero.

Ann Vickers (1933): the private and professional life of a modern woman.

Work of Art (1934): a book about success, its types, varieties, and meaning.

It Can't Happen Here (1935): Lewis's version of how America would become under Fascist dictatorship.

Bethel Merriday (1940): the struggles of a young actress in quest for recognition in the theatrical world.

Cass Timberlane (1945): a novel about marriage.

Kingsblood Royal (1947): an attack on white supremacy in the United States.

NOTES

NOTES